THE
BIG
BOOK OF
ONE POT

THE
BIG
BOOK OF
ONE POT

Love Food ® is an imprint of Parragon Books Ltd

Parragon
Queen Street House
4 Queen Street
Bath BA1 1HE, UK

Copyright © Parragon Books Ltd 2008

Love Food ® and the accompanying heart device is a trademark of Parragon Books Ltd

ISBN 978-1-4075-3969-0

Photography by Mike Cooper
Food styling by Sumi Glass and Lincoln Jefferson
Introduction text by Christine McFadden

All rights reserved. No part of this publication may be reproduced, stored in a retrieval
system or transmitted, in any form or by any means, electronic, mechanical, photocopying,
recording, or otherwise, without the prior permission of the copyright holder.

Printed in China

Notes for the reader
This book uses imperial, metric, and U.S. cup measurements. Follow the same units of
measurement throughout; do not mix imperial and metric. All spoon measurements are
level, unless otherwise stated; teaspoons are assumed to be 5 ml, and tablespoons are
assumed to be 15 ml. Unless otherwise stated, milk is assumed to be whole, eggs and
individual vegetables are medium, and pepper is freshly ground black pepper.

Recipes using raw or lightly cooked eggs should be avoided by infants, the elderly,
pregnant women, convalescents, and anyone with an illness. Pregnant and breastfeeding
women are advised to avoid eating peanuts and peanut products.

Vegetarians should be aware that some brands of the prepared ingredients specified in the
recipes in the Vegetables chapter in this book may contain animal products. Always check
the package before use.

CONTENTS

INTRODUCTION

These days most of us lead action-packed lives, either at work or as a busy parent, or both. Time-consuming meal preparation, let alone clearing up afterward, just doesn't fit in very easily. Yet most of us care about health and want to eat nutritious home-cooked food. What could be more satisfying than something simmering on the stove, filling the air with delicious aromas?

If you love cooking but are short of time, then *The Big Book of One Pot* will be a lifesaver. As the name suggests, all the dishes can be cooked in a single pot with other ingredients, leaving you with very little to wash up but plenty of time to get on with other things.

The one-pot method is a relaxed and flexible way of cooking, easily adjusted to whatever ingredients you have in your refrigerator or pantry. If one ingredient is missing, it's usually possible to substitute another. If you're short of space or equipment, one-pot cooking is ideal— you need just one pot and a single burner.

One-pot cooking doesn't limit you to soups and stews, though this book contains plenty of recipes for these. In many parts of the world, cooking in a single pot is the norm, whether it's a cauldron, a wok, a tagine, or a bean pot. Many dishes grew up out of necessity when food and fuel were scarce. Others were created for religious reasons—the Muslim Ramadan, for example, or the Jewish Sabbath when orthodox believers are forbidden to work or cook. The pot could be left to simmer slowly overnight ready to serve at sunset the following day. In cold climates, it was the conviviality and friendship of communal eating that inspired many one-pot dishes. Think of Swiss fondue, Hungarian goulash, or Mongolian hot pot.

As the recipes in the book demonstrate, this no-frills way of cooking is the ultimate in convenience since everything is ready at the same time. It's the ideal food for solitary suppers or for feeding a crowd. Just put the pot on the table and tuck in.

GETTING STARTED

Although one-pot cooking appears simple, it relies on a certain amount of preplanning to ensure that things go smoothly. More importantly, getting organized from the start means you can relax and enjoy the actual process of cooking instead of running around the kitchen looking for missing utensils or, worse still, discovering too late that you've run out of a vital ingredient.

Before you start to cook:

- Read the recipe all the way through, then plan the sequence according to what needs soaking, chopping, precooking, and so on.
- Have the right tools and cookware at hand
- Make sure knives are sharp
- Wash fresh vegetables, fruits, and herbs
- Assemble all the ingredients then measure or weigh them as necessary
- Complete any preparation beforehand, such as chopping or grating
- Have the prepared ingredients lined up in bowls, ready to add to the pot at the correct time
- Clear up as you go along

USEFUL UTENSILS

As well as basics such as knives and cutting boards, there are a number of additional utensils that make one-pot cooking easier and safer.

Though you can happily leave the pot to simmer while you get on with something else, it's still important to keep track of temperature and time. Thermometers are essential for food safety, and a timer with a loud ring is invaluable for reminding you when the dish needs your attention. You'll also need spoons and spatulas for stirring, and tools for turning and lifting ingredients that are precooked in stages before they go into the pot. A sturdy long-handled fork or multipronged meat lifter are handy for large pieces of meat, while stainless steel spring-action tongs let you clasp smaller pieces of food securely. A perforated shallow skimmer is useful for removing froth and foam from the surface of stews.

Although one-pot recipes are infinitely flexible, it's worth investing in proper measuring spoons and cups, as well as a kitchen scale, especially if you are new to cooking. Once you gain experience and confidence, it's fine to add a pinch of this and a handful of that.

The joy of one-pot meals is that they can be brought straight from oven to table. However, heat can damage unprotected surfaces, so it's a good idea to have a trivet or pot stand at the ready.

COOKWARE

For most of the recipes in this book, a few heavy-bottom saucepans and casseroles in varying sizes with tight-fitting lids make up the basic equipment. You'll also need a high-sided skillet, a wok, good-quality roasting pans that won't warp or twist, and some shallow baking dishes for gratins and crumbles.

FRESH PRODUCE

Wholesome fresh vegetables, meat, poultry, and fish add valuable nutrients to one-pot meals, as well as color, texture, and appetizing flavors.

Vegetables

Vegetables are one of the most important sources of vitamins, minerals, and fiber. They are packed with carotenoids (the plant form of vitamin A), vitamin C, and vitamin E, which collectively protect against heart disease and some cancers.

Meat and poultry

Meat and poultry provide high-quality protein, important minerals such as iron and zinc, and B vitamins, which are needed to release energy from food. Meat tends to be high in fat, so if you're trying to cut down, trim off any excess or choose lean cuts.

Fish and seafood

Dense-fleshed fish and seafood make marvelous one-pot meals. They provide protein and essential minerals, while oily fish such as tuna are a unique source of omega-3 fatty acids that protect against heart disease and feed the brain.

Fresh herbs

A generous sprinkling of fresh herbs added at the end of cooking will provide delightful fragrance and color to one pot meals.

PANTRY ITEMS

A pantry judiciously stocked with a few essentials means you are never without the makings of a one-pot meal.

Grains

Grains such as rice, barley, oats, quinoa, and bulgur wheat contain a range of concentrated nutrients. Perked up with colorful spices and herbs, they form a nutritious base to which meat, fish, and vegetables can be added as necessary.

Beans

Dried beans are packed with nutrients, and provide a mellow background to more strongly flavored ingredients. Canned beans are invaluable since you can add them to the pot without soaking or precooking.

Pasta

Short pasta shapes, from tiny star shapes to coils and fat tubes, make the basis for endless one pot meals. Pasta shapes can be precooked or added to the pot with plenty of liquid.

Seeds and nuts

Crunchy seeds and nuts provide texture and, if chopped finely, can give body to the cooking liquid. Pumpkin, sunflower, and sesame seeds are particularly nutritious, as are walnuts, almonds, and Brazil nuts.

Sauces and pastes

A judicious splash of sauce or dollop of paste can perk up an otherwise bland dish. Soy sauce, Worcestershire sauce, and Tabasco all have outstanding flavors, as do tomato paste, tapenade, and mustards. Ready-made jars of ethnic sauces also add exciting flavors, and save time too.

Spices and dried herbs

For the best flavor, buy spices whole (including pepper) and grind them as needed. Rosemary, thyme, and oregano are the best herbs to use dried; the more delicate varieties are better when fresh. Add spices and dried herbs at the early stages of cooking to bring out the full flavor.

MAKING THE MOST OF THE POT

One-pot meals can be cooked in a variety of pots and pans. Knowing how to get the best from them is invaluable when tackling new recipes.

Casserole

A casserole is ideal for leisurely stews and braises cooked either on the stove or in the oven, and for pot-roasting boned and large rolled pieces of meat. Poultry thighs and drumsticks and dense-fleshed root vegetables are good too. The moist heat encourages a magical exchange of flavors between meat, vegetables, and seasonings, resulting in truly succulent dishes.

After an hour or two with the lid on, test by prodding with a skewer. Meat should feel meltingly tender and root vegetables should be soft but not disintegrating.

High-sided skillet

With a tight-fitting lid and heavy bottom, a high-sided skillet is perfect for slow-cooked rice dishes such as jambalaya, and for braising larger items like chicken quarters or chops. The generous surface area provides maximum contact with heat, enabling meat to brown quickly before adding other ingredients. The contents can then be covered and left to cook at a leisurely pace.

Wok

Given the wok's conical shape and continuous stirring, the food continually falls back to the center where the heat is at its most intense. Since the ingredients are constantly on the move, much less fat is needed, making this a healthy way of cooking.

It is very important to preheat the wok. You should be able to feel the heat radiating from it when you hold your hand flat above the bottom of the interior. Add the oil only when the wok is really hot.

It is essential to have all the ingredients prepared, ready to add to the wok the minute the oil is at the right heat. It should be almost, but not quite, smoking.

Roasting pan

A good solid roasting pan is ideal for a large piece of meat or poultry cooked alongside vegetables such as onions, potatoes, and parsnips. Orange-fleshed vegetables are particularly delicious—try carrots, pumpkin, and sweet potato. Make sure the vegetables are cut into similar-size pieces so that they cook evenly. Tuck some under the meat for extra flavor. A little stock, wine, or water is all that's needed to keep everything moist.

Some roasting pans are self-basting. They have dimpled lids that encourage moisture to gather and drip evenly over the contents below, resulting in a particularly succulent dish.

A pan that is sturdy enough to use on the stove means you can speed up the cooking by giving the meat a quick sizzle before it goes into the oven. The caramelized sediment will dissolve and flavor the other ingredients once they give up their liquid.

Baking and gratin dishes

These dishes are for food that is baked in the oven with a browned topping of potato, bubbling cheese, or crunchy breadcrumbs—or all three.

Baking dishes are particularly suitable for one-pot meals because they can be brought straight from oven to table, saving on the washing up. They are usually made in attractive shapes and colors.

TOP TIPS FOR PERFECT RESULTS

Once you have tried out a few recipes, you may want to create your own one-pot favorites. It's a good idea to follow a few basic techniques:

- Browning meat and poultry before adding other ingredients will produce an appetizing caramelized crust that will dissolve and add flavor to the rest of the dish.

- Add ingredients in descending order of cooking times, slow-cooking dense items first and quick-cooking items last. That way, your one-pot meal will have appetizing texture.

- Add green vegetables just in time to cook them. They'll keep their bright color and the flavor won't dominate the rest of the dish.

- Best of all is homemade stock, either fresh or frozen. Otherwise use Swiss vegetable bouillon powder—stock cubes can be very salty.

Beef Stock

Makes $7^1/_2$ cups

Ingredients

2 lb 4 oz/1 kg beef marrow bones, sawn into
    3-inch/7.5-cm pieces
1 lb 7 oz/650 g braising beef in a single piece
5 pints water
4 cloves
2 onions, halved
2 celery stalks, coarsely chopped
8 peppercorns
1 bouquet garni

1 Put the bones in a large, heavy pan and put
   the braising beef on top. Pour in the water and
   bring to a boil over low heat. Skim off the
   foam that rises to the surface.

2 Press a clove into each onion half and add to
   the pan with the celery, peppercorns, and
   bouquet garni. Partially cover and simmer
   gently for 3 hours. Remove the stewing beef
   from the pan, partially re-cover, and simmer
   for 1 hour more.

3 Remove the pan from the heat and let cool.
   Strain the stock into a bowl, cover with plastic
   wrap, and chill in the refrigerator for at least
   1 hour and preferably overnight.

4 Remove and discard the layer of fat that has
   set on the surface. Use immediately or freeze
   for up to 6 months.

Chicken Stock

Makes $4^1/_2$ pints

Ingredients

3 lb/1.3 kg chicken wings and necks
2 onions, cut into wedges
7 pints water
2 carrots, coarsely chopped
2 celery stalks, coarsely chopped
10 fresh parsley sprigs
4 fresh thyme sprigs
2 bay leaves
10 black peppercorns

1 Place the chicken and onions in a large,
   heavy pan and cook over low heat, stirring
   frequently, until browned all over.

2 Pour in the water and stir well, scraping up
   any sediment from the base of the pan. Bring
   to a boil and skim off the foam that rises to
   the surface.

3 Add the carrots, celery, parsley, thyme, bay
   leaves, and peppercorns, partially cover the
   pan, and simmer gently, stirring occasionally,
   for 3 hours.

4 Remove the pan from the heat and let cool.
   Strain the stock into a bowl, cover with plastic
   wrap, and chill in the refrigerator for at least
   1 hour and preferably overnight.

5 Remove and discard the layer of fat that has
   set on the surface. Use immediately or freeze
   for up to 6 months.

Fish Stock

Makes 5^2/$_3$ cups

Ingredients
1 lb 7 oz/650 g white fish heads, bones,
  and trimmings
1 onion, sliced
2 celery stalks, chopped
1 carrot, sliced
1 bay leaf
4 fresh parsley sprigs
4 black peppercorns
^{1}/$_2$ lemon, sliced
^{1}/$_2$ cup dry white wine
5^2/$_3$ cups water

1 Cut out and discard the gills from the fish
  heads, then rinse the heads, bones, and
  trimmings. Place them in a large pan.

2 Add the remaining ingredients. Bring to a
  boil and skim off the foam that rises to the
  surface. Lower the heat, cover, and simmer
  for 25 minutes.

3 Remove the pan from the heat and let cool.
  Strain the stock into a bowl, without pressing
  down on the contents of the strainer. Use
  immediately or freeze for up to 3 months.

Vegetable Stock

Makes 8^3/$_4$ cups

Ingredients
2 tbsp sunflower or corn oil
4 oz/115 g onions, finely chopped
4 oz/115 g leeks, finely chopped
4 oz/115 g carrots, finely chopped
4 celery stalks, finely chopped
3 oz/85 g fennel, finely chopped
3 oz/85 g tomatoes, finely chopped
4 pints water
1 bouquet garni

1 Heat the oil in a large, heavy pan. Add the
  onions and leeks and cook over low heat,
  stirring occasionally, for 5 minutes, until
  softened.

2 Add the carrots, celery, fennel, and tomatoes,
  cover, and cook, stirring occasionally, for
  10 minutes. Pour in the water, add the
  bouquet garni, and bring to a boil. Lower the
  heat and simmer for 20 minutes.

3 Remove the pan from the heat and let cool.
  Strain the stock into a bowl. Use immediately
  or freeze for up to 3 months.

SOUPS

CHUNKY VEGETABLE SOUP

Put the carrots, onion, garlic, potatoes, celery, mushrooms, tomatoes, and stock into a large pan. Stir in the bay leaf and herbs. Bring to a boil, then reduce the heat, cover, and let simmer for 25 minutes.

Add the corn and cabbage and return to a boil. Reduce the heat, cover, and simmer for 5 minutes, or until the vegetables are tender. Remove and discard the bay leaf. Season to taste with pepper.

Ladle into warmed bowls and serve at once with crusty bread rolls.

SERVES 6

2 carrots, sliced

1 onion, diced

1 garlic clove, crushed

12 oz/350 g new potatoes, diced

2 celery stalks, sliced

4 oz/115 g button mushrooms, quartered

14 oz/400 g canned chopped tomatoes in tomato juice

2½ cups vegetable stock

1 bay leaf

1 tsp dried mixed herbs or 1 tbsp chopped fresh mixed herbs

½ cup corn kernels, frozen or canned, drained

2 oz/55 g green cabbage, shredded

pepper

crusty whole wheat or white bread rolls, to serve

MINESTRONE

Heat the oil in a large pan. Add the garlic, onions, and prosciutto and cook over medium heat, stirring, for 3 minutes, until slightly softened. Add the red and orange bell peppers and the chopped tomatoes and cook for another 2 minutes, stirring. Stir in the stock, then add the celery, beans, cabbage, peas, and parsley. Season with salt and pepper. Bring to a boil, then lower the heat and simmer for 30 minutes.

Add the vermicelli to the pan. Cook for another 10–12 minutes, or according to the instructions on the package. Remove from the heat and ladle into serving bowls. Garnish with freshly grated Parmesan and serve with fresh crusty bread.

SERVES 4

2 tbsp olive oil

2 garlic cloves, chopped

2 red onions, chopped

2¾ oz/75 g prosciutto, sliced

1 red bell pepper, seeded and chopped

1 orange bell pepper, seeded and chopped

14 oz/400 g canned chopped tomatoes

4 cups vegetable stock

1 celery stalk, trimmed and sliced

14 oz/400 g canned borlotti beans, drained

3½ oz/100 g green leafy cabbage, shredded

2¾ oz/75 g frozen peas, thawed

1 tbsp chopped fresh parsley

2¾ oz/75 g dried vermicelli

salt and pepper

freshly grated Parmesan cheese, to garnish

fresh crusty bread, to serve

FRENCH ONION SOUP

SERVES 6

3 tbsp olive oil

1 lb 8 oz/675 g onions, thinly sliced

4 garlic cloves, 3 chopped and 1 peeled but kept whole

1 tsp sugar

2 tsp chopped fresh thyme

2 tbsp all-purpose flour

½ cup dry white wine

8 cups vegetable stock

6 slices of French bread

3 cups grated Swiss cheese

fresh thyme sprigs, to garnish

Heat the olive oil in a large, heavy-bottom pan, then add the onions and cook, stirring occasionally, for 10 minutes, until they are just beginning to brown. Stir in the chopped garlic, sugar, and thyme, then reduce the heat and cook, stirring occasionally, for 30 minutes, or until the onions are golden brown.

Sprinkle in the flour and cook, stirring, for 1–2 minutes. Stir in the wine. Gradually stir in the stock and bring to a boil, skimming off any foam that rises to the surface, then reduce the heat and simmer for 45 minutes. Meanwhile, toast the bread on both sides under a preheated medium broiler. Rub the toast with the whole garlic clove.

Ladle the soup into 6 flameproof bowls set on a baking sheet. Float a piece of toast in each bowl and divide the grated cheese among them. Place under a preheated medium–hot broiler for 2–3 minutes, or until the cheese has just melted. Garnish with thyme sprigs and serve.

ROASTED VEGETABLE SOUP

Preheat the oven to 375°F/190°C.

Brush a large, shallow baking pan with some of the olive oil. Laying them cut-side down, arrange the tomatoes, bell peppers, zucchini, and eggplant in one layer (use two dishes, if necessary). Tuck the garlic cloves and onion pieces into the gaps and drizzle the vegetables with the remaining olive oil. Season lightly with salt and pepper and sprinkle with the thyme.

Place in the preheated oven and bake, uncovered, for 30–35 minutes, or until soft and browned around the edges. Cool, then scrape out the eggplant flesh and remove the skin from the bell peppers.

Working in batches, put the eggplant and bell pepper flesh, together with the tomatoes, zucchini, garlic, and onions, into a food processor and chop to the consistency of salsa; do not purée. Alternatively, place in a bowl and chop together with a knife.

Combine the stock and chopped vegetable mixture in a saucepan and simmer over medium heat for 20–30 minutes, until all the vegetables are tender and the flavors have completely blended.

Stir in the cream and simmer over low heat for about 5 minutes, stirring occasionally, until hot. Taste and adjust the seasoning, if necessary. Ladle the soup into warmed bowls, garnish with basil, and serve.

SERVES 6

3 tbsp olive oil

1 lb 9 oz/700 g ripe tomatoes, skinned, cored, and halved

3 large yellow bell peppers, seeded and halved

3 zucchini, halved lengthwise

1 small eggplant, halved lengthwise

4 garlic cloves, halved

2 onions, cut into eighths

pinch of dried thyme

4 cups chicken, vegetable, or beef stock

½ cup light cream

salt and pepper

shredded basil leaves, to garnish

SQUASH, SWEET POTATO & GARLIC SOUP

Preheat the oven to 375°F/190°C.

Cut the sweet potato, squash, and shallots in half lengthwise, through to the stem end. Scoop the seeds out of the squash. Brush the cut sides with the oil.

Put the vegetables, cut-side down, in a shallow roasting pan. Add the garlic cloves. Roast in the preheated oven for about 40 minutes, until tender and light brown. Set aside to cool.

When cool, scoop the flesh from the potato and squash halves, and put in a saucepan. Remove the peel from the garlic and shallots and add the soft insides to the other vegetables.

Add the stock and a pinch of salt. Bring just to a boil, reduce the heat, and simmer, partially covered, for about 30 minutes, stirring occasionally, until the vegetables are very tender.

Cool the soup slightly, and then transfer to a food processor or blender and process until smooth, working in batches, if necessary. (If using a food processor, strain off the cooking liquid and reserve. Process the soup solids with enough cooking liquid to moisten them, then combine with the remaining liquid.)

Return the soup to the rinsed-out pan and stir in the cream. Season to taste with salt and pepper, then simmer for 5–10 minutes until completely heated through. Ladle into warmed serving bowls, garnish with pepper and snipped chives, and serve.

SERVES 6–8

1 sweet potato, about 12 oz/350 g

1 acorn squash

4 shallots

2 tbsp olive oil

5–6 garlic cloves, unpeeled

3¾ cups chicken stock

½ cup light cream

salt and pepper

snipped chives, to garnish

VICHYSSOISE

SERVES 6

3 large leeks

3 tbsp butter

1 onion, thinly sliced

1 lb/450 g potatoes, chopped

3½ cups vegetable stock

2 tsp lemon juice

pinch of ground nutmeg

¼ tsp ground coriander

1 bay leaf

1 egg yolk

⅔ cup light cream

salt and pepper

freshly snipped chives, to garnish

Trim the leeks, removing most of the green parts. Slice the white parts of the leeks very finely.

Melt the butter in a saucepan. Add the leeks and onion and cook, stirring occasionally, for about 5 minutes without browning.

Add the potatoes, stock, lemon juice, nutmeg, coriander, and bay leaf to the pan, season to taste with salt and pepper, and bring to a boil. Cover and simmer for about 30 minutes, until all the vegetables are very soft.

Cool the soup a little, remove and discard the bay leaf, and then press through a strainer or process in a food processor or blender until smooth. Pour into a clean pan.

Blend the egg yolk into the cream, add a little of the soup to the mixture, and then whisk it all back into the soup and reheat gently, without boiling. Adjust the seasoning to taste. Cool, transfer to a bowl, cover with plastic wrap, and then chill thoroughly in the refrigerator.

Serve the soup sprinkled with freshly snipped chives.

BEEF GOULASH SOUP

Heat the oil in a large, wide saucepan over medium–high heat. Add the beef and sprinkle with salt and pepper. Cook until lightly browned.

Reduce the heat and add the onions and garlic. Cook for about 3 minutes, stirring frequently, until the onions are softened. Stir in the flour and continue cooking for 1 minute.

Gradually stir in the water and combine well, scraping the bottom of the pan to mix in the flour. Stir in the tomatoes, carrot, pepper, paprika, caraway seeds, oregano, and stock.

Bring just to a boil. Reduce the heat, cover, and simmer gently for about 40 minutes, stirring occasionally, until all the vegetables are tender.

Add the tagliatelle to the soup and simmer for an additional 20 minutes, or until the tagliatelle is cooked.

Taste the soup and adjust the seasoning, if necessary. Ladle into warmed bowls and top each with a tablespoonful of sour cream. Garnish with cilantro and serve.

SERVES 6

1 tbsp olive oil

1 lb 2 oz/500 g fresh lean ground beef

2 onions, finely chopped

2 garlic cloves, finely chopped

2 tbsp all-purpose flour

1 cup water

14 oz/400 g canned chopped tomatoes

1 carrot, finely chopped

8 oz/225 g red bell pepper, roasted, peeled, seeded, and chopped

1 tsp Hungarian paprika

¼ tsp caraway seeds

pinch of dried oregano

4 cups beef stock

2 oz/55 g tagliatelle, broken into small pieces

salt and pepper

sour cream and sprigs of fresh cilantro, to garnish

BEEF & BEAN SOUP

Heat the oil in a large pan over medium heat. Add the onion and garlic and cook, stirring frequently, for 3 minutes, or until softened. Add the bell pepper and carrots and cook for an additional 5 minutes.

Meanwhile, drain the peas, reserving the liquid from the can. Place two thirds of the peas, reserving the remainder, in a food processor or blender with the pea liquid and process until smooth.

Add the ground beef to the pan and cook, stirring constantly to break up any lumps, until well browned. Add the spices and cook, stirring, for 2 minutes. Add the cabbage, tomatoes, stock, and processed peas and season to taste with salt and pepper. Bring to a boil, then reduce the heat, cover, and simmer for 15 minutes, or until the vegetables are tender.

Stir in the reserved peas, cover, and simmer for an additional 5 minutes. Ladle the soup into warmed soup bowls and serve.

SERVES 4

2 tbsp vegetable oil

1 large onion, finely chopped

2 garlic cloves, finely chopped

1 green bell pepper, seeded and sliced

2 carrots, sliced

14 oz/400 g canned black-eyed peas

1 cup ground fresh beef

1 tsp each ground cumin, chili powder, and paprika

¼ head of cabbage, sliced

8 oz/225 g tomatoes, peeled and chopped

2½ cups beef stock

salt and pepper

CHORIZO & RED KIDNEY BEAN SOUP

SERVES 4

2 tbsp olive oil

2 garlic cloves, chopped

2 red onions, chopped

1 red bell pepper, seeded and
  chopped

2 tbsp cornstarch

4 cups vegetable stock

1 lb/450 g potatoes, peeled,
  halved, and sliced

5½ oz/150 g chorizo, sliced

2 zucchini, trimmed and sliced

7 oz/200 g canned red kidney
  beans, drained

½ cup heavy cream

salt and pepper

slices of fresh crusty bread,
  to serve

Heat the oil in a large pan. Add the garlic and onions and cook over medium heat, stirring, for 3 minutes, until slightly softened. Add the bell pepper and cook for another 3 minutes, stirring. In a bowl, mix the cornstarch with enough stock to make a smooth paste and stir it into the pan. Cook, stirring, for 2 minutes. Stir in the remaining stock, then add the potatoes and season with salt and pepper. Bring to a boil, then lower the heat and simmer for 25 minutes, until the vegetables are tender.

Add the chorizo, zucchini, and kidney beans to the pan. Cook for 10 minutes, then stir in the cream and cook for another 5 minutes. Remove from the heat and ladle into serving bowls. Serve with slices of fresh crusty bread.

BACON & LENTIL SOUP

Heat a large, heavy-bottom saucepan or flameproof casserole. Add the bacon and cook over medium heat, stirring, for 4–5 minutes, or until the fat runs. Add the chopped onion, carrots, celery, turnip, and potato and cook, stirring frequently, for 5 minutes.

Add the lentils and bouquet garni and pour in the stock. Bring to a boil, reduce the heat, and simmer for 1 hour, or until the lentils are tender.

Remove and discard the bouquet garni and season the soup to taste with pepper, and with salt if necessary. Ladle into warmed soup bowls and serve.

SERVES 4

1 lb/450 g thick, rindless smoked bacon strips, diced

1 onion, chopped

2 carrots, sliced

2 celery stalks, chopped

1 turnip, chopped

1 large potato, chopped

generous 2¼ cups Puy lentils

1 bouquet garni

4 cups chicken stock

salt and pepper

CHEESE & BACON SOUP

Melt the butter in a large pan over medium heat. Add the garlic and onion and cook, stirring, for 3 minutes, until slightly softened. Add the chopped bacon and leeks and cook for another 3 minutes, stirring.

In a bowl, mix the flour with enough stock to make a smooth paste and stir it into the pan. Cook, stirring, for 2 minutes. Pour in the remaining stock, then add the potatoes. Season with salt and pepper. Bring the soup to a boil, then lower the heat and simmer gently for 25 minutes, until the potatoes are tender and cooked through.

Stir in the cream and cook for 5 minutes, then gradually stir in the cheese until melted. Remove from the heat and ladle into individual serving bowls. Garnish with grated cheddar cheese and serve immediately.

36

SERVES 4

2 tbsp butter

2 garlic cloves, chopped

1 large onion, sliced

9 oz/250 g smoked lean bacon, chopped

2 large leeks, trimmed and sliced

2 tbsp all-purpose flour

4 cups vegetable stock

1 lb/450 g potatoes, chopped

scant ½ cup heavy cream

3 cups grated cheddar cheese, plus extra to garnish

salt and pepper

WONTON SOUP

SERVES 6–8

8 cups chicken stock

2 tsp salt

½ tsp white pepper

2 tbsp finely chopped scallion,
   to serve

1 tbsp chopped cilantro leaves,
   to serve

wontons

6 oz/175 g ground pork,
   not too lean

8 oz/225 g raw shrimp, peeled,
   deveined, and chopped

½ tsp finely chopped fresh ginger

1 tbsp light soy sauce

1 tbsp Chinese rice wine

2 tsp finely chopped scallion

pinch of sugar

pinch of white pepper

dash of sesame oil

30 square wonton wrappers

1 egg white, lightly beaten

For the wonton filling, mix together the pork, shrimp, ginger, soy sauce, rice wine, scallion, sugar, pepper, and sesame oil, and stir well until the texture is thick and pasty. Set aside for at least 20 minutes.

To make the wontons, place a teaspoon of the filling at the center of a wrapper. Brush the edges with a little egg white. Bring the opposite points toward each other and press the edges together, creating a flowerlike shape. Repeat with the remaining wrappers and filling.

To make the soup, bring the stock to a boil and add the salt and pepper. Boil the wontons in the stock for about 5 minutes, or until the wrappers begin to wrinkle around the filling.

To serve, divide the scallion among individual bowls, then spoon in the wontons and soup, and sprinkle with the cilantro.

SAUSAGE & RED CABBAGE SOUP

Heat the oil in a large pan. Add the garlic and onion and cook over medium heat, stirring, for 3 minutes, until slightly softened. Add the leek and cook for another 3 minutes, stirring.

In a bowl, mix the cornstarch with enough stock to make a smooth paste, then stir it into the pan. Cook, stirring, for 2 minutes. Stir in the remaining stock, then add the potatoes and sausages. Season with salt and pepper. Bring to a boil, then lower the heat and simmer for 25 minutes.

Add the red cabbage and black-eyed peas and cook for 10 minutes, then stir in the cream and cook for another 5 minutes. Remove from the heat and ladle into serving bowls. Garnish with ground paprika and serve immediately.

SERVES 4

2 tbsp olive oil

1 garlic clove, chopped

1 large onion, chopped

1 large leek, sliced

2 tbsp cornstarch

4 cups vegetable stock

1 lb/450 g potatoes, sliced

7 oz/200 g skinless sausages, sliced

5½ oz/150 g red cabbage, chopped

7 oz/200 g canned black-eyed peas, drained

½ cup heavy cream

salt and pepper

ground paprika, to garnish

ASIAN
LAMB SOUP

Trim all visible fat from the lamb and slice the meat thinly. Cut the slices into bite-size pieces. Spread the meat in one layer on a plate and sprinkle over the garlic and 1 tablespoon of the soy sauce. Marinate, covered, for at least 10 minutes or up to 1 hour.

Put the stock in a saucepan with the ginger, lemongrass, remaining soy sauce, and the chili paste. Bring just to a boil, reduce the heat, cover, and simmer for 10–15 minutes.

When ready to serve the soup, drop the tomatoes, scallions, bean sprouts, and cilantro leaves into the stock.

Heat the oil in a skillet and add the lamb with its marinade. Stir-fry the lamb just until it is no longer red and divide among the warmed bowls.

Ladle over the hot stock and serve immediately.

SERVES 4

5½ oz/150 g lean tender lamb, such as neck fillet or leg steak

2 garlic cloves, very finely chopped

2 tbsp soy sauce

5 cups chicken stock

1 tbsp grated fresh ginger

2-inch/5-cm piece lemongrass, sliced into very thin rounds

¼ tsp chili paste, or to taste

6–8 cherry tomatoes, quartered

4 scallions, finely sliced

1¾ oz/50 g bean sprouts, snapped in half

2 tbsp cilantro leaves

1 tsp olive oil

CHICKEN-NOODLE SOUP

Put the chicken breasts and water in a pan over high heat and bring to a boil. Lower the heat to its lowest setting and simmer, skimming the surface until no more foam rises. Add the onion, garlic, ginger, peppercorns, cloves, star anise, and a pinch of salt, and continue to simmer for 20 minutes, or until the chicken is tender and cooked through. Meanwhile, grate the carrot along its length on the coarse side of a grater so you get long, thin strips.

Strain the chicken, reserving about 5 cups of stock but discarding any flavoring solids. (At this point you can let the stock cool and refrigerate overnight, so any fat solidifies and can be lifted off and discarded.) Return the stock to the rinsed-out pan with the carrot, celery, baby corn, and scallions, and bring to a boil. Boil until the baby corn are almost tender, then add the noodles and continue boiling for 2 minutes.

Meanwhile, chop the chicken, and add to the pan and continue cooking for about 1 minute longer until the chicken is reheated and the noodles are soft. Add seasoning to taste.

SERVES 4–6

2 skinless chicken breasts

8 cups water

1 onion, unpeeled, cut in half

1 large garlic clove, cut in half

½-inch/1-cm piece fresh ginger, peeled and sliced

4 black peppercorns, lightly crushed

4 cloves

2 star anise

1 carrot, peeled

1 celery stalk, chopped

3½ oz/100 g baby corn, cut in half lengthwise and chopped

2 scallions, finely shredded

4 oz/115 g dried rice vermicelli noodles

salt and pepper

CHICKEN & LEEK SOUP

Heat the oil in a large pan over medium heat, add the onions, carrots, and the 2 coarsely chopped leeks, and cook for 3–4 minutes until just golden brown.

Wipe the chicken inside and out and remove and discard any excess skin and fat.

Put the chicken into the pan with the cooked vegetables and add the bay leaves. Pour in enough cold water just to cover and season well with salt and pepper. Bring to a boil, then reduce the heat, cover, and simmer for 1–1½ hours. Skim off any foam that forms from time to time.

Remove the chicken from the stock, remove and discard the skin, then remove all the meat. Cut the meat into neat pieces.

Strain the stock through a colander, discard the vegetables and bay leaves, and return to the rinsed-out pan. Expect to have 4–5 cups of stock. If you have time, it is a good idea to let the stock cool so that the fat solidifies and can be removed. If not, blot the fat off the surface with paper towels.

Heat the stock to simmering point, add the sliced leeks and prunes to the pan, and heat for about 1 minute. Return the chicken to the pan and heat through. Serve immediately in warmed deep dishes, garnished with the parsley.

SERVES 6–8

2 tbsp olive oil

2 onions, coarsely chopped

2 carrots, coarsely chopped

5 leeks, 2 coarsely chopped, 3 thinly sliced

1 chicken, weighing 3 lb/1.3 kg

2 bay leaves

6 prunes, pitted and sliced

salt and pepper

sprigs of fresh parsley, to garnish

CHICKEN & POTATO SOUP WITH BACON

SERVES 4

1 tbsp butter

2 garlic cloves, chopped

1 onion, sliced

9 oz/250 g smoked lean bacon, chopped

2 large leeks, sliced

2 tbsp all-purpose flour

4 cups chicken stock

1 lb 12 oz/800 g potatoes, chopped

7 oz/200 g skinless chicken breast, chopped

4 tbsp heavy cream

salt and pepper

cooked bacon and sprigs of fresh flat-leaf parsley, to garnish

Melt the butter in a large pan over medium heat. Add the garlic and onion and cook, stirring, for 3 minutes, until slightly softened. Add the chopped bacon and leeks and cook for another 3 minutes, stirring.

In a bowl, mix the flour with enough stock to make a smooth paste and stir it into the pan. Cook, stirring, for 2 minutes. Pour in the remaining stock, then add the potatoes and chicken. Season with salt and pepper. Bring to a boil, then lower the heat and simmer for 25 minutes, until the chicken and potatoes are tender and cooked through.

Stir in the cream and cook for another 2 minutes, then remove from the heat and ladle into serving bowls. Garnish with the cooked bacon and flat-leaf parsley and serve immediately.

THAI CHICKEN-COCONUT SOUP

Put the dried noodles in a large bowl with enough lukewarm water to cover and soak for 20 minutes, until soft. Alternatively, cook according to the package instructions. Drain well and set aside.

Meanwhile, bring the stock to a boil in a large pan over high heat. Lower the heat, add the lemongrass, ginger, lime leaves, and chile, and simmer for 5 minutes. Add the chicken and continue simmering for an additional 3 minutes, or until cooked. Stir in the coconut cream, nam pla, and lime juice, and continue simmering for 3 minutes. Add the bean sprouts and scallions and simmer for an additional 1 minute. Taste and gradually add extra nam pla or lime juice at this point, if needed. Remove and discard the lemongrass stalk.

Divide the noodles among 4 bowls. Bring the soup back to a boil, then ladle into the bowls. The heat of the soup will warm the noodles. To garnish, sprinkle with cilantro leaves.

SERVES 4

4 oz/115 g dried cellophane noodles

5 cups chicken stock or vegetable stock

1 lemongrass stalk, crushed

½-inch/1-cm piece fresh ginger, peeled and very finely chopped

2 fresh kaffir lime leaves, thinly sliced

1 fresh red chile, or to taste, seeded and thinly sliced

2 skinless, boneless chicken breasts, thinly sliced

scant 1 cup coconut cream

about 2 tbsp nam pla (Thai fish sauce)

about 1 tbsp fresh lime juice

scant ½ cup bean sprouts

4 scallions, green parts only, finely sliced

fresh cilantro leaves, to garnish

TURKEY & LENTIL SOUP

SERVES 4

1 tbsp olive oil

1 garlic clove, chopped

1 large onion, chopped

7 oz/200 g white mushrooms, sliced

1 red bell pepper, seeded and chopped

6 tomatoes, skinned, seeded, and chopped

4 cups chicken stock

²⁄₃ cup red wine

3 oz/85 g cauliflower florets

1 carrot, chopped

1 cup red lentils

12 oz/350 g cooked turkey, chopped

1 zucchini, chopped

1 tbsp shredded fresh basil

salt and pepper

sprigs of fresh basil, to garnish

Heat the oil in a large pan. Add the garlic and onion and cook over medium heat, stirring, for 3 minutes, until slightly softened. Add the mushrooms, bell pepper, and tomatoes, and cook for another 5 minutes, stirring. Pour in the stock and red wine, then add the cauliflower, carrot, and red lentils. Season to taste with salt and pepper. Bring to a boil, then lower the heat and simmer for 25 minutes, until the vegetables are tender and cooked through.

Add the turkey and zucchini to the pan and cook for 10 minutes. Stir in the shredded basil and cook for another 5 minutes, then remove from the heat and ladle into serving bowls. Garnish with fresh basil sprigs and serve immediately.

DUCK WITH SCALLION SOUP

Slash the skin of the duck 3 or 4 times with a sharp knife and rub in the curry paste. Cook the duck breasts, skin-side down, in a wok or skillet over high heat for 2–3 minutes. Turn over, reduce the heat, and cook for an additional 3–4 minutes, until cooked through. Lift out and slice thickly. Set aside and keep warm.

Meanwhile, heat the oil in a wok or large skillet and stir-fry half the scallions with the garlic, ginger, carrots, and red bell pepper for 2–3 minutes. Pour in the stock and add the chili sauce, soy sauce, and mushrooms. Bring to a boil, reduce the heat, and simmer for 4–5 minutes.

Ladle the soup into warmed bowls, top with the duck slices, and garnish with the remaining scallions. Serve immediately.

SERVES 4

2 duck breasts, skin on

2 tbsp red curry paste

2 tbsp vegetable oil or peanut oil

bunch of scallions, chopped

2 garlic cloves, crushed

2-inch/5-cm piece fresh ginger, grated

2 carrots, thinly sliced

1 red bell pepper, seeded and cut into strips

4 cups chicken stock

2 tbsp sweet chili sauce

3–4 tbsp Thai soy sauce

14 oz/400 g canned straw mushrooms, drained

SEAFOOD
CHOWDER

Discard any mussels with broken shells or any that refuse
to close when tapped. Rinse and pull off any beards. Put the
mussels in a large heavy-bottom saucepan. Cover tightly and
cook over high heat for about 4 minutes, or until the mussels
open, shaking the pan occasionally. Discard any that remain
closed. When they are cool enough to handle, remove the
mussels from the shells and set aside.

Put the flour in a mixing bowl and very slowly whisk in enough
of the stock to make a thick paste. Whisk in a little more stock to
make a smooth liquid.

Melt the butter in a heavy-bottom saucepan over medium–low
heat. Add the onion, cover, and cook for 3 minutes, stirring
frequently, until it softens.

Add the remaining fish stock and bring to a boil. Slowly whisk
in the flour mixture until well combined and bring back to a boil,
whisking constantly. Add the mussel cooking liquid. Season
with salt, if needed, and pepper. Reduce the heat and simmer,
partially covered, for 15 minutes.

Add the whitefish and the mussels and continue simmering,
stirring occasionally, for about 5 minutes, or until the fish is
cooked and begins to flake.

Stir in the shrimp and cream. Taste and adjust the seasoning.
Simmer for 2–3 minutes longer to heat through. Ladle into
warmed bowls, sprinkle with dill, and serve.

SERVES 6

2 lb 4 oz/1 kg live mussels

4 tbsp all-purpose flour

6¼ cups fish stock

1 tbsp butter

1 large onion, finely chopped

12 oz/350 g skinless whitefish
    fillets, such as cod, sole,
    or haddock

7 oz/200 g cooked or raw peeled
    shrimp

1¼ cups heavy cream

salt and pepper

snipped fresh dill, to garnish

BOUILLABAISSE

SERVES 4

scant ½ cup olive oil

3 garlic cloves, chopped

2 onions, chopped

2 tomatoes, seeded and chopped

2¾ cups fish stock

1¾ cups white wine

1 bay leaf

pinch of saffron threads

2 tbsp chopped fresh basil

2 tbsp chopped fresh parsley

7 oz/200 g live mussels

9 oz/250 g snapper or monkfish fillets

9 oz/250 g haddock fillets, skinned

7 oz/200 g shrimp, peeled and deveined

3½ oz/100 g scallops

salt and pepper

Heat the oil in a large pan over medium heat. Add the garlic and onions and cook, stirring, for 3 minutes. Stir in the tomatoes, stock, wine, bay leaf, saffron, and herbs. Bring to a boil, reduce the heat, cover, and simmer for 30 minutes.

Meanwhile, soak the mussels in lightly salted water for 10 minutes. Scrub the shells under cold running water and pull off any beards. Discard any mussels with broken shells or any that refuse to close when tapped. Put the rest into a large pan with a little water, bring to a boil, and cook over high heat for 4 minutes. Remove from the heat and discard any that remain closed.

When the tomato mixture is cooked, rinse the fish fillets, pat dry, and cut into chunks. Add to the pan and simmer for 5 minutes. Add the mussels, shrimp, and scallops, and season with salt and pepper to taste. Cook for 3 minutes, until the fish is cooked through. Remove from the heat, discard the bay leaf, and ladle into serving bowls.

SALMON & LEEK SOUP

Heat the oil in a large, heavy-bottom saucepan over medium heat. Add the onion and leeks and cook for about 3 minutes until they begin to soften.

Add the potato, stock, water, and bay leaf with a large pinch of salt. Bring to a boil, reduce the heat, cover, and cook gently for about 25 minutes until the vegetables are tender. Remove the bay leaf.

Let the soup cool slightly, then transfer about half of it to a food processor or blender and process until smooth. (If using a food processor, strain off the cooking liquid and reserve. Purée half the soup solids with enough cooking liquid to moisten them, then combine with the remaining liquid.)

Return the processed soup to the saucepan and stir to blend. Reheat gently over medium–low heat.

Season the salmon with salt and pepper and add to the soup. Continue cooking for about 5 minutes, stirring occasionally, until the fish is tender and starts to break up. Stir in the cream, taste, and adjust the seasoning, adding a little lemon juice if desired. Ladle into warmed bowls, garnish with chervil or parsley, and serve.

SERVES 4

1 tbsp olive oil

1 large onion, finely chopped

3 large leeks, including green parts, thinly sliced

1 potato, finely diced

2 cups fish stock

3 cups water

1 bay leaf

10½ oz/300 g skinless salmon fillet, cut into ½-inch/1-cm cubes

⅓ cup heavy cream

fresh lemon juice (optional)

salt and pepper

sprigs of fresh chervil or parsley, to garnish

THAI-STYLE SEAFOOD SOUP

Put the stock in a saucepan with the lemongrass, lime rind, ginger, and chili paste. Bring just to a boil, reduce the heat, cover, and simmer for 10–15 minutes.

Cut the shrimp almost in half lengthwise, keeping the tails intact.

Strain the stock, return to the saucepan, and bring to a simmer. Add the scallions and cook for 2–3 minutes. Taste and season with salt, if needed, and stir in a little more chili paste if desired.

Add the scallops and shrimp and poach for about 1 minute until they turn opaque and the shrimp curl.

Stir in the fresh cilantro leaves, ladle the soup into warmed bowls, dividing the shellfish evenly, and garnish with chiles.

SERVES 4

5 cups fish stock

1 lemongrass stalk, split lengthwise

pared rind of ½ lime, or 1 lime leaf

1-inch/2.5-cm piece fresh ginger, sliced

¼ tsp chili paste, or to taste

7 oz/200 g large or medium raw shrimp, peeled

4–6 scallions, sliced

9 oz/250 g scallops

2 tbsp fresh cilantro leaves

salt

finely sliced red chiles, to garnish

MEAT

POT ROAST
WITH POTATOES
& DILL

Preheat the oven to 275°F/140°C. Mix 2 tablespoons of the flour with the salt and pepper in a shallow dish. Dip the meat to coat. Heat the oil in a flameproof casserole and brown the meat all over. Transfer to a plate. Add half the butter to the casserole and cook the onion, celery, carrots, dill seeds, and thyme for 5 minutes. Return the meat and juices to the casserole.

Pour in the wine and enough stock to reach one-third of the way up the meat. Bring to a boil, cover, and cook in the oven for 3 hours, turning the meat every 30 minutes. After it has been cooking for 2 hours, add the potatoes and more stock if necessary.

When ready, transfer the meat and vegetables to a warmed serving dish. Strain the cooking liquid to remove any solids, then return the liquid to the casserole.

Mix the remaining butter and flour to a paste. Bring the cooking liquid to a boil. Whisk in small pieces of the flour and butter paste, whisking constantly until the sauce is smooth. Pour the sauce over the meat and vegetables. Sprinkle with the fresh dill to serve.

SERVES 6

2½ tbsp all-purpose flour

1 tsp salt

¼ tsp pepper

1 rolled brisket of beef, weighing 3 lb 8 oz/1.6 kg

2 tbsp vegetable oil

2 tbsp butter

1 onion, finely chopped

2 celery stalks, diced

2 carrots, peeled and diced

1 tsp dill seeds

1 tsp dried thyme or oregano

1½ cups red wine

⅔–1 cup beef stock

4–5 potatoes, cut into large chunks and boiled until just tender

2 tbsp chopped fresh dill, to serve

BEEF
STROGANOFF

Place the dried porcini mushrooms in a bowl and cover with hot water. Let soak for 20 minutes. Meanwhile, cut the beef against the grain into ¼-inch/5-mm thick slices, then into ½-inch/1-cm long strips, and reserve.

Drain the mushrooms, reserving the soaking liquid, and chop. Strain the soaking liquid through a fine-mesh strainer or coffee filter and reserve.

Heat half the oil in a large skillet. Add the shallots and cook over low heat, stirring occasionally, for 5 minutes, or until softened. Add the dried mushrooms, reserved soaking water, and whole cremini mushrooms and cook, stirring frequently, for 10 minutes, or until almost all of the liquid has evaporated, then transfer the mixture to a plate.

Heat the remaining oil in the skillet, add the beef and cook, stirring frequently, for 4 minutes, or until browned all over. You may need to do this in batches. Return the mushroom mixture to the skillet and season to taste with salt and pepper. Place the mustard and cream in a small bowl and stir to mix, then fold into the mixture. Heat through gently, then serve with freshly cooked pasta, garnished with chives.

SERVES 4

½ oz/15 g dried porcini mushrooms

12 oz/350 g beef tenderloin

2 tbsp olive oil

4 oz/115 g shallots, sliced

6 oz/175 g cremini mushrooms

½ tsp Dijon mustard

5 tbsp heavy cream

salt and pepper

freshly cooked pasta, to serve

fresh chives, to garnish

CHILI CON CARNE

SERVES 4

1 lb 10 oz/750 g lean braising beef

2 tbsp vegetable oil

1 large onion, sliced

2–4 garlic cloves, crushed

1 tbsp all-purpose flour

generous 1¾ cups tomato juice

14 oz/400 g canned tomatoes

1–2 tbsp sweet chili sauce

1 tsp ground cumin

15 oz/425 g canned red kidney
    beans, drained and rinsed

½ tsp dried oregano

1–2 tbsp chopped fresh parsley

salt and pepper

sprigs of fresh herbs, to garnish

freshly cooked rice and tortillas,
    to serve

Preheat the oven to 325°F/160°C. Using a sharp knife, cut the beef into ¾-inch/2-cm cubes. Heat the vegetable oil in a large flameproof casserole and cook the beef over medium heat until well seared on all sides. Remove the beef from the casserole with a slotted spoon and set aside until ready to use.

Add the onion and garlic to the casserole and cook until lightly browned, then stir in the flour and cook for 1–2 minutes.

Stir in the tomato juice and tomatoes and bring to a boil. Return the beef to the casserole and add the chili sauce, cumin, and salt and pepper to taste. Cover and cook in the preheated oven for 1½ hours, or until the beef is almost tender.

Stir in the kidney beans, oregano, and parsley, and adjust the seasoning to taste, if necessary. Cover the casserole and return to the oven for 45 minutes. Transfer to 4 large, warmed serving plates, garnish with sprigs of fresh herbs, and serve immediately with freshly cooked rice and tortillas.

MEAT

81

BEEF GOULASH

Heat the vegetable oil in a large pan and cook the onion and garlic for 3–4 minutes.

Cut the braising beef into chunks and cook over high heat for 3 minutes until browned all over. Add the paprika and stir well, then add the chopped tomatoes, tomato paste, bell pepper, and mushrooms. Cook for 2 minutes, stirring frequently.

Pour in the beef stock. Bring to a boil, then reduce the heat. Cover and simmer for 1½–2 hours until the meat is tender.

Blend the cornstarch with the water, then add to the pan, stirring until thickened and smooth. Cook for 1 minute, then season with salt and pepper to taste.

Put the yogurt in a serving bowl and sprinkle with a little paprika.

Transfer the beef goulash to a warmed serving dish, garnish with chopped fresh parsley, and serve with the yogurt and freshly cooked long-grain and wild rice.

SERVES 4

2 tbsp vegetable oil

1 large onion, chopped

1 garlic clove, crushed

1 lb 10 oz/750 g lean braising beef

2 tbsp paprika

15 oz/425 g can chopped tomatoes

2 tbsp tomato paste

1 large red bell pepper, seeded and chopped

6 oz/175 g button mushrooms, sliced

2½ cups beef stock

1 tbsp cornstarch

1 tbsp water

salt and pepper

4 tbsp lowfat plain yogurt

paprika, for sprinkling

chopped fresh parsley, to garnish

freshly cooked long-grain and wild rice, to serve

BEEF WITH HERBS & VEGETABLES

Preheat the oven to 375°F/190°C. To make the stock, trim as much fat as possible from the beef and put in a large roasting pan with the bones and onions. Roast for 30–40 minutes until browned, turning once or twice. Transfer the ingredients to a large flameproof casserole and discard the fat.

Add the water (it should cover by at least 2 inches/5 cm) and bring to a boil. Skim off any foam that rises to the surface. Reduce the heat and add the garlic, carrots, leek, celery, bay leaf, thyme, and a pinch of salt. Simmer very gently, uncovered, for 4 hours, skimming occasionally. Do not stir. If the ingredients emerge from the liquid, top up with water.

Gently ladle the stock through a cheesecloth-lined sieve into a large container and remove as much fat as possible. Save the meat for another purpose, if desired, and discard the bones and vegetables. (There should be about 8 cups of stock.)

Boil the stock very gently until it is reduced to 6¼ cups, or if the stock already has concentrated flavor, measure out that amount and save the rest for another purpose. Taste the stock and adjust the seasoning if necessary.

Bring a saucepan of salted water to a boil and drop in the celeriac and carrots. Reduce the heat, cover, and boil gently for about 15 minutes until tender. Drain.

Add the marjoram and parsley to the boiling beef stock. Divide the cooked vegetables and diced tomatoes among warmed bowls, ladle over the boiling stock, and serve.

SERVES 4–6

7 oz/200 g celeriac, peeled and finely diced

2 large carrots, finely diced

2 tsp chopped fresh marjoram leaves

2 tsp chopped fresh parsley

2 plum tomatoes, skinned, seeded, and diced

salt and pepper

beef stock

1 lb 4 oz/550 g boneless beef shin or braising beef, cut into large cubes

1 lb 10 oz/750 g veal, beef, or pork bones

2 onions, quartered

10 cups water

4 garlic cloves, sliced

2 carrots, sliced

1 large leek, sliced

1 celery stick, chopped

1 bay leaf

4–5 sprigs of fresh thyme, or ¼ tsp dried thyme

salt

PEPPER POT-STYLE STEW

SERVES 4

1 lb/450 g braising beef

1½ tbsp all-purpose flour

2 tbsp olive oil

1 red onion, chopped

3–4 garlic cloves, crushed

1 fresh green chile, seeded and chopped

3 celery stalks, sliced

4 whole cloves

1 tsp ground allspice

1–2 tsp hot pepper sauce, or to taste

2½ cups beef stock

8 oz/225 g seeded and peeled squash, such as acorn, cut into small chunks

1 large red bell pepper, seeded and chopped

4 tomatoes, coarsely chopped

4 oz/115 g okra, trimmed and halved

freshly cooked wild rice, to serve

Trim any fat or gristle from the beef and cut the meat into 1-inch/2.5-cm chunks. Toss the beef in the flour until well coated and reserve any remaining flour.

Heat the oil in a large, heavy-bottom pan and cook the onion, garlic, chile, and celery with the cloves and allspice, stirring frequently, for 5 minutes or until softened. Add the beef and cook over high heat, stirring frequently, for 3 minutes, or until browned on all sides and seared. Sprinkle in the reserved flour and cook, stirring constantly, for 2 minutes, then remove from the heat.

Add the hot pepper sauce and gradually stir in the stock, then return to the heat and bring to a boil, stirring. Reduce the heat, then cover and simmer, stirring occasionally, for 1½ hours.

Add the squash and red bell pepper to the pan and simmer for an additional 15 minutes. Add the tomatoes and okra and simmer for an additional 15 minutes, or until the beef is tender. Serve with the wild rice.

BEEF & VEGETABLE STEW

Trim any fat or gristle from the beef and cut the meat into 1-inch/2.5-cm chunks. Mix the flour and spices together. Toss the beef in the spiced flour until well coated.

Heat the oil in a large, heavy-bottom pan and cook the onion, garlic, and celery, stirring frequently, for 5 minutes or until softened. Add the beef and cook over high heat, stirring frequently, for 3 minutes, or until browned on all sides and seared.

Add the carrots, then remove from the heat. Gradually stir in the lager and stock, then return to the heat and bring to a boil, stirring. Reduce the heat, then cover and simmer, stirring occasionally, for 1½ hours.

Add the potatoes to the pan and simmer for an additional 15 minutes. Add the red bell pepper and corn cobs and simmer for 15 minutes, then add the tomatoes and peas and simmer for an additional 10 minutes, or until the beef and vegetables are tender. Season to taste with salt and pepper, then stir in the cilantro and serve.

SERVES 4

1 lb/450 g braising beef

1½ tbsp all-purpose flour

1 tsp hot paprika

1–1½ tsp chili powder

1 tsp ground ginger

2 tbsp olive oil

1 large onion, cut into chunks

3 garlic cloves, sliced

2 celery stalks, sliced

8 oz/225 g carrots, chopped

1¼ cups lager

1¼ cups beef stock

12 oz/350 g potatoes, chopped

1 red bell pepper, seeded and chopped

2 corn cobs, halved

4 oz/115 g tomatoes, cut into quarters

1 cup shelled fresh or frozen peas

salt and pepper

1 tbsp chopped fresh cilantro

RICH BEEF STEW

Combine the wine, brandy, vinegar, shallots, carrots, garlic, peppercorns, thyme, rosemary, parsley, and bay leaf, and season to taste with salt. Add the beef, stirring to coat, then cover with plastic wrap and marinate in the refrigerator for 8 hours, or overnight.

Preheat the oven to 300°F/150°C. Drain the beef, reserving the marinade, and pat dry on paper towels. Heat half the oil in a large, flameproof casserole. Add the beef cubes in batches and cook over medium heat, stirring, for 3–4 minutes, or until browned. Transfer the beef to a plate with a slotted spoon. Brown the remaining beef, adding more oil, if necessary.

Return all of the beef to the casserole and add the tomatoes and their juices, mushrooms, and orange rind. Strain the reserved marinade into the casserole. Bring to a boil, cover, and cook in the oven for 2½ hours.

Remove the casserole from the oven, add the prosciutto and olives, and return it to the oven to cook for an additional 30 minutes, or until the beef is very tender. Discard the orange rind and serve straight from the casserole, garnished with parsley.

SERVES 6

1½ cups dry white wine

2 tbsp brandy

1 tbsp white wine vinegar

4 shallots, sliced

4 carrots, sliced

1 garlic clove, finely chopped

6 black peppercorns

4 fresh thyme sprigs

1 fresh rosemary sprig

2 fresh parsley sprigs, plus extra to garnish

1 bay leaf

1 lb 10 oz/750 g top round steak, cut into 1-inch/2.5-cm cubes

2 tbsp olive oil

1 lb 12 oz/800 g canned chopped tomatoes

8 oz/225 g portobello mushrooms, sliced

strip of finely pared orange rind

2 oz/55 g prosciutto, cut into strips

12 black olives

salt

BEEF IN BEER WITH HERB DUMPLINGS

SERVES 6

2 tbsp corn oil

2 large onions, thinly sliced

8 carrots, sliced

4 tbsp all-purpose flour

2 lb 12 oz/1.25 kg braising beef, cut into cubes

generous 1¾ cups stout

2 tsp brown sugar

2 bay leaves

1 tbsp chopped fresh thyme

salt and pepper

herb dumplings

generous ¾ cup self-rising flour

pinch of salt

½ cup lard, chilled and cut into small pieces

2 tbsp chopped fresh parsley, plus extra to garnish

about 4 tbsp water

Preheat the oven to 325°F/160°C. Heat the oil in a flameproof casserole. Add the onions and carrots and cook over low heat, stirring occasionally, for 5 minutes, or until the onions are softened. Meanwhile, place the flour in a plastic bag and season with salt and pepper. Add the braising beef to the bag, tie the top, and shake well to coat. Do this in batches, if necessary.

Remove the vegetables from the casserole with a slotted spoon and reserve. Add the braising beef to the casserole, in batches, and cook, stirring frequently, until browned all over. Return all the meat and the onions and carrots to the casserole and sprinkle in any remaining seasoned flour. Pour in the stout and add the sugar, bay leaves, and thyme. Bring to a boil, cover, and transfer to the preheated oven to bake for 1¾ hours.

To make the herb dumplings, sift the flour and salt into a bowl. Stir in the suet and parsley and add enough of the water to make a soft dough. Shape into small balls between the palms of your hands. Add to the casserole and return to the oven for 30 minutes. Remove and discard the bay leaves and serve, sprinkled with parsley.

BEEF CHOP SUEY

Combine all the marinade ingredients in a bowl and marinate the beef for at least 20 minutes. Blanch the broccoli in a large pan of boiling water for 30 seconds. Drain and set aside.

In a preheated wok or deep skillet, heat 1 tablespoon of the oil and stir-fry the beef until the color has changed. Remove and set aside. Wipe out the wok or skillet with paper towels.

In the clean wok or deep pan, heat the remaining oil and stir-fry the onion for 1 minute. Add the celery and broccoli and cook for 2 minutes. Add the snow peas, bamboo shoots, water chestnuts, and mushrooms, and cook for 1 minute. Add the beef, then season with the oyster sauce and salt and serve.

SERVES 4

1 lb/450 g porterhouse steak, thinly sliced

1 head of broccoli, cut into small florets

2 tbsp vegetable oil or peanut oil

1 onion, thinly sliced

2 celery stalks, thinly sliced diagonally

2 cups snow peas, sliced in half lengthwise

½ cup fresh or canned bamboo shoots, rinsed and julienned (if using fresh shoots, boil in water first for 30 minutes)

8 water chestnuts, thinly sliced

4 cups thinly sliced button mushrooms

1 tbsp oyster sauce

1 tsp salt

marinade

1 tbsp Chinese rice wine

pinch of white pepper

pinch of salt

1 tbsp light soy sauce

½ tsp sesame oil

POT-ROAST PORK

Heat the oil with half the butter in a heavy-bottomed pan or flameproof casserole. Add the pork and cook over medium heat, turning frequently, for 5–10 minutes, or until browned. Transfer to a plate.

Add the shallots to the pan and cook, stirring frequently, for 5 minutes, or until softened. Add the juniper berries and thyme sprigs and return the pork to the pan, with any juices that have collected on the plate. Pour in the cider and stock, season to taste with salt and pepper, then cover and simmer for 30 minutes. Turn the pork over and add the celery. Re-cover the pan and cook for an additional 40 minutes.

Meanwhile, make a beurre manié by mashing the remaining butter with the flour in a small bowl. Transfer the pork and celery to a platter with a slotted spoon and keep warm. Remove and discard the juniper berries and thyme. Whisk the beurre manié, a little at a time, into the simmering cooking liquid. Cook, stirring constantly, for 2 minutes, then stir in the cream and bring to a boil.

Slice the pork and spoon a little of the sauce over it. Garnish with thyme sprigs and serve immediately with the celery, peas, and remaining sauce.

SERVES 4

1 tbsp corn oil

¼ cup butter

2 lb 4 oz/1 kg boned and rolled pork loin

4 shallots, chopped

6 juniper berries

2 fresh thyme sprigs, plus extra to garnish

⅔ cup hard cider

⅔ cup chicken stock or water

8 celery stalks, chopped

2 tbsp all-purpose flour

⅔ cup heavy cream

salt and pepper

freshly cooked peas, to serve

PORK & VEGETABLE BROTH

SERVES 4

1 tbsp chili oil

1 garlic clove, chopped

3 scallions, sliced

1 red bell pepper, seeded and finely sliced

2 tbsp cornstarch

4 cups vegetable stock

1 tbsp soy sauce

2 tbsp rice wine or dry sherry

5½ oz/150 g pork tenderloin, sliced

1 tbsp finely chopped lemongrass

1 small red chile, seeded and finely chopped

1 tbsp grated fresh ginger

4 oz/115 g fine egg noodles

7 oz/200 g canned water chestnuts, drained and sliced

salt and pepper

Heat the oil in a large pan. Add the garlic and scallions and cook over medium heat, stirring, for 3 minutes, until slightly softened. Add the bell pepper and cook for an additional 5 minutes, stirring.

In a bowl, mix the cornstarch with enough of the stock to make a smooth paste and stir it into the pan. Cook, stirring, for 2 minutes. Stir in the remaining stock with the soy sauce and rice wine, then add the pork, lemongrass, chile, and ginger. Season with salt and pepper. Bring to a boil, then lower the heat and simmer for 25 minutes.

Bring a separate pan of water to a boil, add the noodles, and cook for 3 minutes. Remove from the heat, drain, then add the noodles to the soup along with the water chestnuts. Cook for another 2 minutes, then remove from the heat and ladle into serving bowls.

PORK CHOPS WITH BELL PEPPERS & CORN

Heat the oil in a large, flameproof casserole. Add the pork chops in batches and cook over medium heat, turning occasionally, for 5 minutes, or until browned. Transfer the chops to a plate with a slotted spoon.

Add the chopped onion to the casserole and cook, stirring occasionally, for 5 minutes, or until softened. Add the garlic and bell peppers and cook, stirring occasionally, for an additional 5 minutes. Stir in the corn kernels and their juices and the parsley and season to taste.

Return the chops to the casserole, spooning the vegetable mixture over them. Cover and simmer for 30 minutes, or until tender. Serve immediately with mashed potatoes.

SERVES 4

1 tbsp corn oil

4 pork chops, trimmed of visible fat

1 onion, chopped

1 garlic clove, finely chopped

1 green bell pepper, seeded and sliced

1 red bell pepper, seeded and sliced

11½ oz/325 g canned corn kernels

1 tbsp chopped fresh parsley

salt and pepper

mashed potatoes, to serve

PORK & VEGETABLE STEW

Trim off any fat or gristle from the pork and cut the meat into thin strips about 2-inches/5-cm long. Mix the flour and spices together. Toss the pork in the spiced flour until well coated and reserve any remaining spiced flour.

Heat the oil in a large, heavy-bottom pan and cook the onion, stirring frequently, for 5 minutes, or until softened. Add the pork and cook over high heat, stirring frequently, for 5 minutes, or until browned on all sides and seared. Sprinkle in the reserved spiced flour and cook, stirring constantly, for 2 minutes, then remove from the heat.

Gradually add the tomatoes to the pan. Blend the tomato paste with a little of the stock in a pitcher and gradually stir into the pan, then stir in half the remaining stock.

Add the carrots, then return to the heat and bring to a boil, stirring. Reduce the heat, then cover and simmer, stirring occasionally, for 1½ hours. Add the squash and cook for an additional 15 minutes.

Add the leeks and okra, and the remaining stock if you prefer a thinner stew. Simmer for an additional 15 minutes, or until the pork and vegetables are tender. Season to taste with salt and pepper, then garnish with fresh parsley and serve with couscous.

SERVES 4

1 lb/450 g lean boneless pork

1½ tbsp all-purpose flour

1 tsp ground coriander

1 tsp ground cumin

1½ tsp ground cinnamon

1 tbsp olive oil

1 onion, chopped

14 oz/400 g canned chopped tomatoes

2 tbsp tomato paste

1¼–scant 2 cups chicken stock

8 oz/225 g carrots, chopped

12 oz/350 g squash, such as kabocha, peeled, seeded, and chopped

8 oz/225 g leeks, sliced, blanched, and drained

4 oz/115 g okra, trimmed and sliced

salt and pepper

sprigs of fresh parsley, to garnish

couscous, to serve

PORK WITH RED CABBAGE

SERVES 4

1 tbsp corn oil

1 lb 10 oz/750 g boned and rolled pork loin

1 onion, finely chopped

1 lb 2 oz/500 g red cabbage, thick stems removed and leaves shredded

2 large cooking apples, peeled, cored, and sliced

3 cloves

1 tsp brown sugar

3 tbsp lemon juice, and a thinly pared strip of lemon rind

lemon wedges, to garnish

Preheat the oven to 325°F/160°C. Heat the oil in a flameproof casserole. Add the pork and cook over medium heat, turning frequently, for 5–10 minutes, until browned. Transfer to a plate.

Add the chopped onion to the casserole and cook over low heat, stirring occasionally, for 5 minutes, or until softened. Add the cabbage, in batches, and cook, stirring, for 2 minutes. Transfer each batch (mixed with some onion) into a bowl with a slotted spoon.

Add the apple slices, cloves, and sugar to the bowl and mix well, then place about half the mixture in the bottom of the casserole. Top with the pork, then add the remaining cabbage mixture. Sprinkle in the lemon juice and add the strip of rind. Cover and cook in the preheated oven for 1½ hours.

Transfer the pork to a plate. Transfer the cabbage mixture to the plate with a slotted spoon and keep warm. Bring the cooking juices to a boil over high heat and reduce slightly. Slice the pork and arrange on warmed serving plates, surrounded with the cabbage mixture. Spoon the cooking juices over the meat and serve with wedges of lemon.

MEAT

105

PAPRIKA PORK

Cut the pork into 1½-inch/4-cm cubes. Heat the oil and butter in a large pan. Add the pork and cook over medium heat, stirring, for 5 minutes, or until browned. Transfer to a plate with a slotted spoon.

Add the chopped onion to the pan and cook, stirring occasionally, for 5 minutes, or until softened. Stir in the paprika and flour and cook, stirring constantly, for 2 minutes. Gradually stir in the stock and bring to a boil, stirring constantly.

Return the pork to the pan, add the sherry and sliced mushrooms, and season to taste with salt and pepper. Cover and simmer gently for 20 minutes, or until the pork is tender. Stir in the sour cream and serve.

SERVES 4

1 lb 8 oz/675 g pork tenderloin

2 tbsp corn oil

2 tbsp butter

1 onion, chopped

1 tbsp paprika

2½ tbsp all-purpose flour

1¼ cups chicken stock, or
   1 chicken bouillon cube
   dissolved in 1¼ cups boiling
   water

4 tbsp dry sherry

4 oz/115 g button mushrooms,
   sliced

salt and pepper

⅔ cup sour cream

ASIAN PORK

SERVES 4

1 lb/450 g lean boneless pork

1½ tbsp all-purpose flour

1–2 tbsp olive oil

1 onion, cut into small wedges

2–3 garlic cloves, chopped

1-inch/2.5-cm piece fresh ginger,
    peeled and grated

1 tbsp tomato paste

1¼ cups chicken stock

8 oz/225 g canned pineapple
    chunks in natural juice

1–1½ tbsp dark soy sauce

1 red bell pepper, seeded and
    sliced

1 green bell pepper, seeded and
    sliced

1½ tbsp balsamic vinegar

4 scallions, diagonally sliced,
    to garnish

Trim off any fat or gristle from the pork and cut the meat into
1-inch/2.5-cm chunks. Toss the pork in the flour until well
coated and reserve any remaining flour.

Heat the oil in a large, heavy-bottom pan and cook the
onion, garlic, and ginger, stirring frequently, for 5 minutes,
or until softened. Add the pork and cook over high heat,
stirring frequently, for 5 minutes, or until browned on all sides
and seared. Sprinkle in the reserved flour and cook, stirring
constantly, for 2 minutes, then remove from the heat.

Blend the tomato paste with the stock in a heatproof pitcher
and gradually stir into the pan. Drain the pineapple, reserving
both the fruit and juice, and stir the juice into the pan.

Add the soy sauce to the pan, then return to the heat and
bring to a boil, stirring. Reduce the heat, then cover and simmer,
stirring occasionally, for 1 hour. Add the bell peppers and cook
for an additional 15 minutes, or until the pork is tender. Stir in
the vinegar and the reserved pineapple and heat through for
5 minutes. Serve sprinkled with the scallions.

SPICED PORK WITH BELL PEPPERS

Heat the oil in a wok or large skillet and sauté the onion and garlic for 1–2 minutes, until they are softened but not browned.

Add the pork slices and stir-fry for 2–3 minutes until browned all over. Add the bell pepper, mushrooms, and curry paste.

Dissolve the coconut in the stock and add to the wok with the soy sauce. Bring to a boil and then simmer for 4–5 minutes until the liquid has reduced and thickened.

Add the tomatoes and cilantro and cook for 1–2 minutes before serving with noodles.

SERVES 4

2 tbsp vegetable oil or peanut oil

1 onion, coarsely chopped

2 garlic cloves, chopped

1 lb/450 g pork tenderloin, thickly sliced

1 red bell pepper, seeded and cut into squares

6 oz/175 g button mushrooms, quartered

2 tbsp Thai red curry paste

4 oz/115 g block creamed coconut, chopped

1¼ cups pork stock or vegetable stock

2 tbsp Thai soy sauce

4 tomatoes, peeled, seeded, and chopped

handful of fresh cilantro, chopped

boiled noodles or rice, to serve

LAMB SHANKS
WITH HARISSA

Preheat the oven to 400°F/200°C. Prick the eggplants, place on a baking sheet, and bake for 1 hour. When cool, peel and chop.

Heat the oil in a large saucepan. Add the lamb and cook until browned. Add the onion, stock, and water. Bring to a boil. Reduce the heat and simmer for 1 hour.

For the harissa, process the bell peppers, coriander seeds, chiles, garlic, and caraway seeds in a food processor. With the motor running, add enough oil to make a paste. Season with salt, then spoon into a jar. Cover with oil, seal, and chill.

Remove the shanks from the stock, cut off the meat, and chop. Add the sweet potato, cinnamon, and cumin to the stock, bring to a boil, cover, and simmer for 20 minutes. Discard the cinnamon and process the mixture in a food processor with the eggplant. Return to the pan, add the lamb and cilantro, and heat until hot. Serve with the harissa.

SERVES 4

2 eggplants

3 tbsp olive oil

6 lamb shanks

1 small onion, chopped

1¾ cups chicken stock

8 cups water

14 oz/400 g sweet potato, cut into chunks

2-inch/5-cm piece cinnamon stick

1 tsp ground cumin

2 tbsp chopped fresh cilantro

harissa

2 red bell peppers, peeled, seeded, and chopped

½ tsp coriander seeds, dry-roasted

1 oz/25 g fresh red chiles, chopped

2 garlic cloves, chopped

2 tsp caraway seeds

olive oil

salt

LAMB PILAU

SERVES 4

2–3 tbsp vegetable oil

1 lb 7 oz/650 g boneless lamb
   shoulder, cut into 1-inch/2.5-cm
   cubes

2 onions, coarsely chopped

1 tsp ground cumin

7 oz/200 g risotto rice

1 tbsp tomato paste

1 tsp saffron threads

scant ½ cup pomegranate juice

scant 3½ cups lamb stock, chicken
   stock, or water

4 oz/115 g dried apricots or
   prunes, halved

2 tbsp raisins

2 tbsp shredded fresh mint

2 tbsp shredded fresh watercress

salt and pepper

Heat the oil in a large flameproof casserole or pan over high heat. Add the lamb, in batches, and cook over high heat, turning frequently, for 7 minutes, or until lightly browned.

Add the onions, reduce the heat to medium, and cook for 2 minutes, or until beginning to soften. Add the cumin and rice and cook, stirring to coat, for 2 minutes, or until the rice is translucent. Stir in the tomato paste and the saffron threads.

Add the pomegranate juice and stock. Bring to a boil, stirring. Stir in the apricots and raisins. Reduce the heat to low, cover, and simmer for 20–25 minutes, or until the lamb and rice are tender and all of the liquid has been absorbed.

Season to taste with salt and pepper, then sprinkle the shredded mint and watercress over the pilaf and serve straight from the casserole.

LAMB WITH PEARS

Preheat the oven to 325°F/160°C. Heat the olive oil in a flameproof casserole over medium heat. Add the lamb and cook, turning frequently, for 5–10 minutes, or until browned on all sides.

Arrange the pear pieces on top, then sprinkle over the ginger. Cover with the potatoes. Pour in the cider and season to taste with salt and pepper. Cover and cook in the preheated oven for 1¼ hours.

Trim the stem ends of the green beans. Remove the casserole from the oven and add the beans, then re-cover and return to the oven for an additional 30 minutes. Taste and adjust the seasoning and sprinkle with the chives. Serve immediately.

SERVES 4

1 tbsp olive oil

2 lb 4 oz/1 kg best end-of-neck lamb cutlets, trimmed of visible fat

6 pears, peeled, cored, and cut into quarters

1 tsp ground ginger

4 potatoes, diced

4 tbsp hard cider

1 lb/450 g green beans

salt and pepper

2 tbsp snipped fresh chives, to garnish

CINNAMON LAMB CASSEROLE

Season the flour with salt and pepper to taste and put it with the lamb in a plastic bag, then hold the top closed and shake until the lamb cubes are lightly coated all over. Remove the lamb from the bag, then shake off any excess flour and set aside.

Heat the oil in a large, flameproof casserole and cook the onions and garlic, stirring frequently, for 5 minutes, or until softened. Add the lamb and cook over high heat, stirring frequently, for 5 minutes, or until browned on all sides and seared.

Stir the wine, vinegar, and tomatoes and their juice into the casserole, scraping any sediment from the bottom of the casserole, and bring to a boil. Reduce the heat and add the raisins, cinnamon, sugar, and bay leaf. Season to taste with salt and pepper. Cover and simmer gently for 2 hours, or until the lamb is tender.

Meanwhile, make the topping. Put the yogurt into a small serving bowl, then stir in the garlic and season to taste with salt and pepper. Cover and chill in the refrigerator until ready to serve.

Discard the bay leaf and serve the lamb hot, topped with a spoonful of the garlic yogurt, and dusted with paprika.

SERVES 6

2 tbsp all-purpose flour

2 lb 4 oz/1 kg lean boneless lamb, cubed

2 tbsp olive oil

2 large onions, sliced

1 garlic clove, finely chopped

1¼ cups full-bodied red wine

2 tbsp red wine vinegar

14 oz/400 g canned chopped tomatoes

generous ⅓ cup seedless raisins

1 tbsp ground cinnamon

pinch of sugar

1 bay leaf

salt and pepper

paprika, to garnish

topping

⅔ cup plain yogurt

2 garlic cloves, crushed

salt and pepper

LAMB STEW WITH CHICKPEAS

SERVES 4–6

6 tbsp olive oil

8 oz/225 g chorizo sausage, cut into ¼-inch/5-mm thick slices, casings removed

2 large onions, chopped

6 large garlic cloves, crushed

2 lb/900 g boned leg of lamb, cut into 2-inch/5-cm chunks

scant 1¼ cups lamb stock or water

½ cup red wine, such as Rioja or Tempranillo

2 tbsp sherry vinegar

1 lb 12 oz/800 g canned chopped tomatoes

4 sprigs fresh thyme, plus extra to garnish

2 bay leaves

½ tsp sweet Spanish paprika

1 lb 12 oz/800 g canned chickpeas, rinsed and drained

salt and pepper

Heat 4 tablespoons of the oil in a large, heavy-bottom flameproof casserole over medium-high heat. Reduce the heat, add the chorizo, and cook for 1 minute; set aside. Add the onions to the casserole and cook for 2 minutes, then add the garlic and continue cooking for 3 minutes, or until the onions are soft, but not brown. Remove from the casserole and set aside.

Heat the remaining 2 tablespoons of oil in the casserole. Add the lamb chunks in a single layer without overcrowding the casserole, and cook until browned on all sides; work in batches, if necessary.

Return the onion mixture to the casserole with all the lamb. Stir in the stock, wine, vinegar, tomatoes with their juices, and salt and pepper to taste. Bring to a boil, scraping any glazed bits from the bottom of the casserole. Reduce the heat and stir in the thyme, bay leaves, and paprika.

Transfer to a preheated oven, 325°F/160°C, and cook, covered, for 40–45 minutes until the lamb is tender. Stir in the chickpeas and return to the oven, uncovered, for 10 minutes, or until they are heated through and the juices are reduced.

Taste and adjust the seasoning. Garnish with thyme and serve.

SPICY LAMB & CHICKPEA STEW

Heat 1 tablespoon of the oil in a large saucepan or cast-iron casserole over medium–high heat. Cut the lamb into cubes and add to the pan, in batches if necessary to avoid overcrowding, and cook until evenly browned on all sides, adding a little more oil if needed. Remove the meat with a slotted spoon when browned.

Reduce the heat and add the onion and garlic to the pan. Cook, stirring frequently, for 1–2 minutes.

Add the water and return all the meat to the pan. Bring just to a boil and skim off any foam that rises to the surface. Reduce the heat and stir in the tomatoes, bay leaf, thyme, oregano, cinnamon, cumin, turmeric, and harissa. Simmer for about 1 hour, or until the meat is very tender. Discard the bay leaf.

Rinse and drain the chickpeas, then stir into the pan with the carrot and potato and simmer for 15 minutes. Add the zucchini and peas and continue simmering for 15–20 minutes, or until all the vegetables are tender.

Adjust the seasoning, adding more harissa, if desired. Ladle the soup into warmed bowls and garnish with mint or cilantro.

SERVES 4–6

1–2 tbsp olive oil

1 lb/450 g lean boneless lamb

1 onion, finely chopped

2–3 garlic cloves, crushed

5 cups water

14 oz/400 g canned chopped tomatoes

1 bay leaf

½ tsp each dried thyme and oregano

⅛ tsp ground cinnamon

¼ tsp each ground cumin and turmeric

1 tsp harissa, or more to taste

14 oz/400 g canned chickpeas

1 carrot, diced

1 potato, diced

1 zucchini, quartered lengthwise and sliced

3½ oz/100 g fresh or defrosted frozen peas

salt and pepper

sprigs of fresh mint or cilantro, to garnish

IRISH STEW

Preheat the oven to 325°F/160°C. Spread the flour on a plate and season with salt and pepper. Roll the pieces of lamb in the flour to coat, shaking off any excess, and arrange in the bottom of a casserole.

Layer the onions, carrots, and potatoes on top of the lamb.

Sprinkle in the thyme and pour in the stock, then cover and cook in the preheated oven for 2½ hours. Garnish with the chopped parsley and serve straight from the casserole.

SERVES 4

4 tbsp all-purpose flour

3 lb/1.3 kg middle neck of lamb, trimmed of visible fat, cut into chunks

3 large onions, chopped

3 carrots, sliced

1 lb/450 g potatoes, cut into quarters

½ tsp dried thyme

scant 3½ cups hot beef stock

salt and pepper

2 tbsp chopped fresh parsley, to garnish

HEARTY WINTER BROTH

Heat the vegetable oil in a large, heavy-bottom saucepan and add the pieces of lamb, turning them to sear and brown on both sides. Lift the lamb out of the pan and set aside until ready to use.

Add the onion, carrots, and leeks to the saucepan and cook gently for about 3 minutes.

Return the lamb to the saucepan and add the vegetable stock, bay leaf, parsley, and pearl barley to the saucepan. Bring the mixture in the pan to a boil, then reduce the heat. Cover and simmer for 1½ –2 hours.

Discard the parsley sprigs and the bay leaf. Lift the pieces of lamb from the broth and let them cool slightly. Remove the bones and any fat and chop the meat. Return the lamb to the broth and reheat gently. Season to taste with salt and pepper.

It is advisable to prepare this soup a day ahead, then leave it to cool, cover, and refrigerate overnight. When ready to serve, remove and discard the layer of fat from the surface and reheat the soup gently. Ladle into warmed bowls and serve immediately.

SERVES 4

1 tbsp vegetable oil

1 lb 2 oz/500 g lean neck of lamb, cut into chunks

1 large onion, sliced

2 carrots, sliced

2 leeks, sliced

4 cups vegetable stock

1 bay leaf

sprigs of fresh parsley

2 oz/55 g pearl barley

salt and pepper

OSSO BUCCO

Heat the oil and butter in a large, heavy-bottom skillet. Add the onions and leek and cook over low heat, stirring occasionally, for 5 minutes, until softened.

Spread out the flour on a plate and season with salt and pepper. Toss the slices of veal in the flour to coat, shaking off any excess. Add the veal to the skillet, increase the heat to high, and cook until browned on both sides.

Gradually stir in the wine and stock and bring just to a boil, stirring constantly. Reduce the heat, cover, and simmer for 1¼ hours, or until the veal is very tender.

Meanwhile, make the gremolata by mixing the parsley, garlic, and lemon rind in a small bowl.

Transfer the veal to a warmed serving dish with a slotted spoon. Bring the sauce to a boil and cook, stirring occasionally, until thickened and reduced. Pour the sauce over the veal, sprinkle with the gremolata, and serve immediately.

SERVES 4

1 tbsp virgin olive oil

4 tbsp butter

2 onions, chopped

1 leek, sliced

3 tbsp all-purpose flour

4 thick slices of veal shin (osso bucco)

1¼ cups white wine

1¼ cups veal stock or chicken stock

salt and pepper

gremolata

2 tbsp chopped fresh parsley

1 garlic clove, finely chopped

grated rind of 1 lemon

POULTRY

ITALIAN-STYLE ROAST CHICKEN

Rinse the chicken inside and out with cold water and drain well. Carefully cut between the skin and the top of the breast meat using a small pointed knife. Slide a finger into the slit and carefully enlarge it to form a pocket. Continue until the skin is completely lifted away from both breasts and the top of the legs.

Chop the leaves from 3 rosemary stems. Mix with the feta cheese, sun-dried tomato paste, butter, and pepper to taste, then spoon under the skin. Put the chicken in a large roasting pan, cover with foil, and cook in a preheated oven, 375°F/190°C, for 20 minutes per 1 lb 2 oz/500 g, plus 20 minutes.

Break the garlic bulb into cloves but do not peel. Add the vegetables and garlic to the chicken after 40 minutes, drizzle with oil, tuck in a few stems of rosemary, and season with salt and pepper. Cook for the remaining calculated time, removing the foil for the last 40 minutes to brown the chicken.

Transfer the chicken to a serving platter. Place some of the vegetables around the chicken and transfer the remainder to a warmed serving dish. Spoon the fat (it will be floating on top) out of the roasting pan and stir the flour into the remaining cooking juices. Place the roasting pan on top of the stove and cook over medium heat for 2 minutes, then gradually stir in the stock. Bring to a boil, stirring, until thickened. Strain into a sauce boat and serve with the chicken.

SERVES 6

5 lb 8 oz/2.5 kg chicken

sprigs of fresh rosemary

¾ cup coarsely grated feta cheese

2 tbsp sun-dried tomato paste

4 tbsp butter, softened

1 bulb garlic

2 lb 4 oz/1 kg new potatoes, halved if large

1 each red, green, and yellow bell pepper, seeded and cut into chunks

3 zucchini, thinly sliced

2 tbsp olive oil

2 tbsp all-purpose flour

2½ cups chicken stock

salt and pepper

CHICKEN IN WHITE WINE

Preheat the oven to 325°F/160°C. Melt half the butter with the oil in a flameproof casserole. Add the bacon and cook over medium heat, stirring, for 5–10 minutes, or until golden brown. Transfer the bacon to a large plate. Add the onions and garlic to the casserole and cook over low heat, stirring occasionally, for 10 minutes, or until golden. Transfer to the plate. Add the chicken and cook over medium heat, stirring constantly, for 8–10 minutes, or until golden. Transfer to the plate.

Drain off any excess fat from the casserole. Stir in the wine and stock and bring to a boil, scraping any sediment off the bottom. Add the bouquet garni and season to taste. Return the bacon, onions, and chicken to the casserole. Cover and cook in the preheated oven for 1 hour. Add the mushrooms, re-cover, and cook for 15 minutes. Meanwhile, make a beurre manié by mashing the remaining butter with the flour in a small bowl.

Remove the casserole from the oven and set over medium heat. Remove and discard the bouquet garni. Whisk in the beurre manié, a little at a time. Bring to a boil, stirring constantly, then serve, garnished with fresh herb sprigs.

SERVES 4

¼ cup butter

2 tbsp olive oil

2 thick, rindless, lean bacon strips, chopped

4 oz/115 g pearl onions, peeled

1 garlic clove, finely chopped

4 lb/1.8 kg chicken pieces

1¾ cups dry white wine

1¼ cups chicken stock

1 bouquet garni

4 oz/115 g button mushrooms

2½ tbsp all-purpose flour

salt and pepper

fresh mixed herbs, to garnish

COQ AU VIN

SERVES 4

¼ cup butter

2 tbsp olive oil

4 lb/1.8 kg chicken pieces

4 oz/115 g rindless smoked bacon,
  cut into strips

4 oz/115 g pearl onions, peeled

4 oz/115 g cremini mushrooms,
  halved

2 garlic cloves, finely chopped

2 tbsp brandy

scant 1 cup red wine

1¼ cups chicken stock

1 bouquet garni

2 tbsp all-purpose flour

salt and pepper

bay leaves, to garnish

Melt half the butter with the olive oil in a large, flameproof casserole. Add the chicken and cook over medium heat, stirring, for 8–10 minutes, or until golden brown. Add the bacon, onions, mushrooms, and garlic.

Pour in the brandy and set it alight with a match or taper. When the flames have died down, add the wine, stock, and bouquet garni, and season to taste with salt and pepper. Bring to a boil, reduce the heat, and simmer gently for 1 hour, or until the chicken pieces are cooked through and tender. Meanwhile, make a beurre manié by mashing the remaining butter with the flour in a small bowl.

Remove and discard the bouquet garni. Transfer the chicken to a large plate and keep warm. Stir the beurre manié into the casserole, a little at a time. Bring to a boil, return the chicken to the casserole, and serve immediately, garnished with bay leaves.

SPICED CHICKEN STEW

POULTRY

Season the chicken pieces with salt and dust with paprika.

Heat the oil and butter in a flameproof casserole or large pan. Add the chicken pieces and cook over medium heat, turning, for 10–15 minutes, or until golden. Transfer to a plate with a slotted spoon.

Add the onion and bell peppers to the casserole. Cook over low heat, stirring occasionally, for 5 minutes, or until softened. Add the tomatoes, wine, stock, Worcestershire sauce, Tabasco sauce, and parsley and bring to a boil, stirring. Return the chicken to the casserole, cover, and simmer, stirring occasionally, for 30 minutes.

Add the corn and beans to the casserole, partially re-cover, and simmer for an additional 30 minutes. Place the flour and water in a small bowl and mix to make a paste. Stir a ladleful of the cooking liquid into the paste, then stir it into the stew. Cook, stirring frequently, for 5 minutes. Serve, garnished with parsley.

SERVES 6

4 lb/1.8 kg chicken pieces

2 tbsp paprika

2 tbsp olive oil

2 tbsp butter

1 lb/450 g onions, chopped

2 yellow bell peppers, seeded and chopped

14 oz/400 g canned chopped tomatoes

scant 1 cup dry white wine

generous 1¾ cups chicken stock

1 tbsp Worcestershire sauce

½ tsp Tabasco sauce

1 tbsp finely chopped fresh parsley

11½ oz/325 g canned corn kernels, drained

15 oz/425 g canned lima beans, drained and rinsed

2 tbsp all-purpose flour

4 tbsp water

salt

fresh parsley sprigs, to garnish

HUNTER'S
CHICKEN

Preheat the oven to 325°F/160°C. Heat the butter and oil in a flameproof casserole and cook the chicken over medium–high heat, turning frequently, for 10 minutes, or until golden all over and seared. Using a slotted spoon, transfer to a plate.

Add the onions and garlic to the casserole and cook over low heat, stirring occasionally, for 10 minutes, or until softened and golden. Add the tomatoes with their juice, the herbs, sun-dried tomato paste, and wine, and season to taste with salt and pepper. Bring to a boil, then return the chicken portions to the casserole, pushing them down into the sauce.

Cover and cook in the preheated oven for 50 minutes. Add the mushrooms and cook for an additional 10 minutes, or until the chicken is tender and the juices run clear when a skewer is inserted into the thickest part of the meat. Serve immediately.

SERVES 4

1 tbsp unsalted butter

2 tbsp olive oil

4 lb/1.8 kg skinned chicken portions

2 red onions, sliced

2 garlic cloves, finely chopped

14 oz/400 g canned chopped tomatoes

2 tbsp chopped fresh flat-leaf parsley

6 fresh basil leaves, torn

1 tbsp sun-dried tomato paste

⅔ cup red wine

8 oz/225 g button mushrooms, sliced

salt and pepper

SUNSHINE CHICKEN

SERVES 4

1 lb/450 g skinless, boneless chicken

1½ tbsp all-purpose flour

1 tbsp olive oil

1 onion, cut into wedges

2 celery stalks, sliced

⅔ cup orange juice

1¼ cups chicken stock

1 tbsp light soy sauce

1–2 tsp clear honey

1 tbsp grated orange rind

1 orange bell pepper, seeded and chopped

8 oz/225 g zucchini, sliced into half moons

2 small corn cobs, halved, or 3½ oz/100 g baby corn

1 orange, peeled and segmented

salt and pepper

1 tbsp chopped fresh parsley, to garnish

Lightly rinse the chicken and pat dry with paper towels. Cut into bite-size pieces. Season the flour well with salt and pepper. Toss the chicken in the seasoned flour until well coated and reserve any remaining seasoned flour.

Heat the oil in a large, heavy-bottom skillet and cook the chicken over high heat, stirring frequently, for 5 minutes, or until golden on all sides and seared. Using a slotted spoon, transfer to a plate.

Add the onion and celery to the skillet and cook over medium heat, stirring frequently, for 5 minutes, or until softened. Sprinkle in the reserved seasoned flour and cook, stirring constantly, for 2 minutes, then remove from the heat. Gradually stir in the orange juice, stock, soy sauce, and honey followed by the orange rind, then return to the heat and bring to a boil, stirring.

Return the chicken to the skillet. Reduce the heat, then cover and simmer, stirring occasionally, for 15 minutes. Add the orange bell pepper with the zucchini and corn cobs and simmer for an additional 10 minutes, or until the chicken and vegetables are tender. Add the orange segments, then stir well and heat through for 1 minute. Serve garnished with the parsley.

CHICKEN & BARLEY STEW

Heat the oil in a large pot over medium heat. Add the chicken and cook for 3 minutes, then turn over and cook on the other side for another 2 minutes. Add the stock, barley, potatoes, carrots, leek, shallots, tomato paste, and bay leaf. Bring to a boil, lower the heat, and simmer for 30 minutes.

Add the zucchini and chopped parsley, cover the pan, and cook for another 20 minutes, or until the chicken is cooked through. Remove the bay leaf and discard.

In a separate bowl, mix the flour with 4 tablespoons of water and stir into a smooth paste. Add it to the stew and cook, stirring, over low heat for another 5 minutes. Season to taste with salt and pepper.

Remove from the heat, ladle into individual serving bowls, and garnish with sprigs of fresh parsley.

SERVES 4

2 tbsp vegetable oil

8 small, skinless chicken thighs

generous 2 cups chicken stock

scant ½ cup pearl barley, rinsed and drained

7 oz/200 g small new potatoes, scrubbed and cut in half lengthwise

2 large carrots, peeled and sliced

1 leek, trimmed and sliced

2 shallots, sliced

1 tbsp tomato paste

1 bay leaf

1 zucchini, trimmed and sliced

2 tbsp chopped fresh flat-leaf parsley, plus extra sprigs to garnish

2 tbsp all-purpose flour

4 tbsp water

salt and pepper

CHICKEN WITH GARLIC

Sift the flour onto a large plate and season with paprika and salt and pepper to taste. Dredge the chicken pieces with the flour on both sides, shaking off the excess.

Heat 4 tablespoons of the oil in a large, deep skillet or flameproof casserole over medium heat. Add the garlic and cook, stirring frequently, for about 2 minutes to flavor the oil. Remove with a slotted spoon and set aside to drain on paper towels.

Add as many chicken pieces, skin-side down, as will fit in a single layer. (Work in batches if necessary, to avoid overcrowding the skillet, adding a little extra oil if necessary.) Cook for 5 minutes until the skin is golden brown. Turn over and cook for 5 minutes longer.

Pour off any excess oil. Return the garlic and chicken pieces to the skillet and add the chicken stock, wine, and herbs. Bring to a boil, then reduce the heat, cover, and simmer for 20–25 minutes, until the chicken is cooked through and tender and the garlic is very soft.

Transfer the chicken pieces to a serving platter and keep them warm. Bring the cooking liquid to a boil, with the garlic and herbs, and boil until reduced to about 1½ cups. Remove and discard the herbs. Taste and adjust the seasoning, if necessary.

Spoon the sauce and the garlic cloves over the chicken pieces. Garnish with the parsley and thyme, and serve.

SERVES 6

4 tbsp all-purpose flour

Spanish paprika, either hot or smoked sweet, to taste

1 large chicken, about 3 lb 12 oz/ 1.7 kg, cut into 8 pieces, then rinsed

4–6 tbsp olive oil

24 large garlic cloves, peeled and halved

scant 2 cups chicken stock

4 tbsp dry white wine, such as white Rioja

2 sprigs of fresh parsley, 1 bay leaf, and 1 sprig of fresh thyme, tied together

salt and pepper

fresh parsley and thyme leaves, to garnish

SPICY CHICKEN WITH VEGETABLES

SERVES 4

5 tbsp corn oil

4 chicken pieces

6 tbsp all-purpose flour

1 onion, chopped

2 celery stalks, sliced

1 green bell pepper, seeded
   and chopped

2 garlic cloves, finely chopped

2 tsp chopped fresh thyme

2 fresh red chiles, seeded
   and finely chopped

14 oz/400 g canned chopped
   tomatoes

1¼ cups chicken stock

salt and pepper

lamb's lettuce and chopped fresh
   thyme, to garnish

Heat the oil in a large, heavy-bottom saucepan or flameproof casserole. Add the chicken and cook over medium heat, stirring, for 5–10 minutes or until golden. Transfer the chicken to a plate with a slotted spoon.

Stir the flour into the oil and cook over very low heat, stirring constantly, for 15 minutes, or until light golden. Do not let it burn. Immediately add the onion, celery, and green bell pepper and cook, stirring constantly, for 2 minutes. Add the garlic, thyme, and chiles and cook, stirring, for 1 minute.

Stir in the tomatoes and their juices, then gradually stir in the stock. Return the chicken pieces to the pan, cover, and simmer for 45 minutes, or until the chicken is cooked through and tender. Season to taste with salt and pepper, transfer to warmed serving plates, and serve immediately, garnished with some lamb's lettuce and a sprinkling of chopped thyme.

CHICKEN TAGINE

Heat the oil in a large pan over medium heat, add the onion and garlic and cook for 3 minutes, stirring frequently. Add the chicken and cook, stirring constantly, for an additional 5 minutes, or until seared on all sides. Add the cumin and cinnamon sticks to the pan halfway through searing the chicken.

Sprinkle in the flour and cook, stirring constantly, for 2 minutes. Add the eggplant, red bell pepper, and mushrooms and cook for an additional 2 minutes, stirring constantly.

Blend the tomato paste with the stock, stir into the pan, and bring to a boil. Reduce the heat and add the chickpeas and apricots. Cover and let simmer for 15–20 minutes, or until the chicken is tender.

Season with salt and pepper to taste and serve at once, sprinkled with cilantro.

SERVES 4

1 tbsp olive oil

1 onion, cut into small wedges

2–4 garlic cloves, sliced

1 lb/450 g skinless, boneless chicken breast, diced

1 tsp ground cumin

2 cinnamon sticks, lightly bruised

1 tbsp whole wheat flour

8 oz/225 g eggplant, diced

1 red bell pepper, seeded and chopped

3 oz/85 g button mushrooms, sliced

1 tbsp tomato paste

2½ cups chicken stock

10 oz/280 g canned chickpeas, drained and rinsed

⅓ cup no-soak dried apricots, chopped

salt and pepper

1 tbsp chopped fresh cilantro, to garnish

BALTI CHICKEN

Heat the ghee in a large, heavy-bottom skillet. Add the onions and cook over low heat, stirring occasionally, for 10 minutes, or until golden. Add the sliced tomatoes, nigella seeds, peppercorns, cardamom, cinnamon stick, chili powder, garam masala, garlic paste, and ginger paste, and season with salt to taste. Cook, stirring constantly, for 5 minutes.

Add the chicken and cook, stirring constantly, for 5 minutes, or until well coated in the spice paste. Stir in the yogurt. Cover and let simmer, stirring occasionally, for 10 minutes.

Stir in the chopped cilantro, chiles, and lime juice. Transfer to a warmed serving dish, sprinkle with more chopped cilantro, and serve immediately.

SERVES 6

3 tbsp ghee or vegetable oil

2 large onions, sliced

3 tomatoes, sliced

½ tsp nigella seeds

4 black peppercorns

2 cardamom pods

1 cinnamon stick

1 tsp chili powder

1 tsp garam masala

1 tsp garlic paste

1 tsp ginger paste

1 lb 9 oz/700 g skinless, boneless chicken breasts or thighs, diced

2 tbsp plain yogurt

2 tbsp chopped fresh cilantro, plus extra to garnish

2 fresh green chiles, seeded and finely chopped

2 tbsp lime juice

salt

SPICY AROMATIC CHICKEN

SERVES 4

4–8 chicken pieces, skinned

½ lemon, cut into wedges

4 tbsp olive oil

1 onion, coarsely chopped

2 large garlic cloves, finely
    chopped

½ cup dry white wine

14 oz/400 g canned chopped
    tomatoes in juice

pinch of sugar

½ tsp ground cinnamon

½ tsp ground cloves

½ tsp ground allspice

14 oz/400 g canned artichoke
    hearts or okra, drained

8 black olives, pitted

salt and pepper

Rub the chicken pieces with the lemon. Heat the oil in a large, flameproof casserole or lidded skillet. Add the onion and garlic and cook for 5 minutes, until softened. Add the chicken pieces and cook for 5–10 minutes, until browned on all sides.

Pour in the wine and add the tomatoes with their juice, along with the sugar, cinnamon, cloves, allspice, and salt and pepper and bring to a boil. Cover the casserole and simmer for 45 minutes to 1 hour, until the chicken is tender.

Meanwhile, if using artichoke hearts, cut them in half. Add the artichokes and the olives to the casserole 10 minutes before the end of cooking, and continue to simmer until heated through. Serve hot.

165

THAI GREEN CHICKEN CURRY

Heat the oil in a preheated wok or large, heavy-bottom skillet. Add 2 tablespoons of the curry paste and stir-fry briefly until all the aromas are released.

Add the chicken, lime leaves, and lemongrass and stir-fry for 3–4 minutes, until the meat is starting to color. Add the coconut milk and eggplants and let simmer gently for 8–10 minutes, or until tender.

Stir in the fish sauce and serve at once, garnished with Thai basil sprigs and lime leaves.

SERVES 4

2 tbsp peanut oil or corn oil

2 tbsp Thai green curry paste

1 lb 2 oz/500 g skinless boneless chicken breasts, cut into cubes

2 kaffir lime leaves, coarsely torn

1 lemongrass stalk, finely chopped

1 cup canned coconut milk

16 baby eggplants, halved

2 tbsp Thai fish sauce

fresh Thai basil sprigs and thinly sliced kaffir lime leaves, to garnish

CHICKEN JALFREZI

Grind the cumin and coriander seeds in a mortar with a pestle, then reserve. Heat the mustard oil in a large, heavy-bottom skillet over high heat for 1 minute, or until it begins to smoke. Add the vegetable oil, reduce the heat, and add the onion and garlic. Cook for 10 minutes, or until golden.

Add the tomato paste, chopped tomatoes, turmeric, ground cumin and coriander seeds, chili powder, garam masala, and vinegar to the skillet. Stir the mixture until fragrant.

Add the red bell pepper and fava beans and stir for an additional 2 minutes, or until the bell pepper is softened. Stir in the chicken, and season to taste with salt, then simmer gently for 6–8 minutes, until the chicken is heated through and the beans are tender. Transfer to warmed serving bowls, garnish with cilantro sprigs, and serve with freshly cooked rice.

SERVES 4

½ tsp cumin seeds

½ tsp coriander seeds

1 tsp mustard oil

3 tbsp vegetable oil

1 large onion, finely chopped

3 garlic cloves, crushed

1 tbsp tomato paste

2 tomatoes, peeled and chopped

1 tsp ground turmeric

½ tsp chili powder

½ tsp garam masala

1 tsp red wine vinegar

1 small red bell pepper, seeded and chopped

4½ oz/125 g frozen fava beans

1 lb 2 oz/500 g cooked chicken, chopped

salt

fresh cilantro sprigs, to garnish

freshly cooked rice, to serve

JAMBALAYA

SERVES 4

2 tbsp vegetable oil

2 onions, coarsely chopped

1 green bell pepper, seeded and
   coarsely chopped

2 celery stalks, coarsely chopped

3 garlic cloves, finely chopped

2 tsp paprika

10½ oz/300 g skinless, boneless
   chicken breasts, chopped

3½ oz/100 g andouille or other
   smoked sausage, chopped

3 tomatoes, peeled and chopped

2 cups long-grain rice

3¾ cups hot chicken stock
   or fish stock

1 tsp dried oregano

2 bay leaves

12 large jumbo shrimp

4 scallions, finely chopped

2 tbsp chopped fresh parsley

salt and pepper

chopped fresh herbs, to garnish

Heat the vegetable oil in a large skillet over low heat. Add the
onions, bell pepper, celery, and garlic and cook for 8–10 minutes
until all the vegetables have softened. Add the paprika and cook
for another 30 seconds. Add the chicken and sausages and cook
for 8–10 minutes until lightly browned. Add the tomatoes and
cook for 2–3 minutes until they have collapsed.

Add the rice to the pan and stir well. Pour in the hot stock,
oregano, and bay leaves, and stir well. Cover and simmer
for 10 minutes.

Add the shrimp and stir well. Cover again and cook for
another 6–8 minutes until the rice is tender and the shrimp
are cooked through.

Stir in the scallions and parsley, and season to taste with
salt and pepper. Transfer to a large serving dish, garnish with
chopped fresh herbs, and serve.

ITALIAN TURKEY CUTLETS

Heat the oil in a flameproof casserole or heavy-bottom skillet. Add the turkey scallops and cook over medium heat for 5–10 minutes, turning occasionally, until golden. Transfer to a plate.

Seed and slice the red bell peppers. Slice the onion, add to the skillet with the bell peppers, and cook over low heat, stirring occasionally, for 5 minutes, or until softened. Add the garlic and cook for an additional 2 minutes.

Return the turkey to the skillet and add the strained tomatoes, wine, and marjoram. Season to taste. Bring to a boil, then reduce the heat, cover, and simmer, stirring occasionally, for 25–30 minutes, or until the turkey is cooked through and tender.

Stir in the cannellini beans. Simmer for an additional 5 minutes. Sprinkle the breadcrumbs over the top and place under a preheated medium-hot broiler for 2–3 minutes, or until golden. Serve, garnished with basil.

SERVES 4

1 tbsp olive oil

4 turkey scallops or steaks

2 red bell peppers

1 red onion

2 garlic cloves, finely chopped

1¼ cups strained tomatoes

⅔ cup medium white wine

1 tbsp chopped fresh marjoram

14 oz/400 g canned cannellini beans, drained and rinsed

3 tbsp fresh white breadcrumbs

salt and pepper

fresh basil sprigs, to garnish

SPICED TURKEY

Preheat the oven to 325°F/160°C. Spread the flour on a plate and season with salt and pepper. Coat the turkey fillets in the seasoned flour, shaking off any excess.

Heat the oil in a flameproof casserole. Add the turkey fillets and cook over medium heat, turning occasionally, for 5–10 minutes, or until golden. Transfer to a plate with a slotted spoon.

Add the onion and bell pepper to the casserole. Cook over low heat, stirring occasionally, for 5 minutes, or until softened. Sprinkle in any remaining seasoned flour and cook, stirring constantly, for 1 minute. Gradually stir in the stock, then add the raisins, chopped tomatoes, chili powder, cinnamon, cumin, and chocolate. Season to taste with salt and pepper. Bring to a boil, stirring constantly.

Return the turkey to the casserole, cover, and cook in the preheated oven for 50 minutes. Serve immediately, garnished with sprigs of cilantro.

SERVES 4

6 tbsp all-purpose flour

4 turkey breast fillets

3 tbsp corn oil

1 onion, thinly sliced

1 red bell pepper, seeded and sliced

1¼ cups chicken stock

2 tbsp raisins

4 tomatoes, peeled, seeded, and chopped

1 tsp chili powder

½ tsp ground cinnamon

pinch of ground cumin

1 oz/25 g semisweet chocolate, finely chopped or grated

salt and pepper

sprigs of fresh cilantro, to garnish

DUCK LEGS
WITH OLIVES

SERVES 4

4 duck legs, all visible fat trimmed off

1 lb 12 oz/800 g canned tomatoes, chopped

8 garlic cloves, peeled but left whole

1 large onion, chopped

1 carrot, peeled and finely chopped

1 celery stalk, peeled and finely chopped

3 sprigs fresh thyme

generous ½ cup Spanish green olives in brine, stuffed with pimientos, garlic, or almonds, drained and rinsed

1 tsp finely grated orange rind

salt and pepper

Put the duck legs in the bottom of a flameproof casserole or a large, heavy-bottom skillet with a tight-fitting lid. Add the tomatoes, garlic, onion, carrot, celery, thyme, and olives, and stir together. Season with salt and pepper to taste.

Turn the heat to high and cook, uncovered, until the ingredients start to bubble. Reduce the heat to low, cover tightly, and let simmer for 1¼–1½ hours, until the duck is very tender. Check occasionally and add a little water if the mixture appears to be drying out.

When the duck is tender, transfer it to a serving platter, cover, and keep hot in a preheated warm oven. Leave the casserole uncovered, increase the heat to medium, and cook, stirring, for about 10 minutes until the mixture forms a sauce. Stir in the orange rind, then taste and adjust the seasoning if necessary.

Mash the tender garlic cloves with a fork and spread over the duck legs. Spoon the sauce over the top. Serve at once.

DUCK JAMBALAYA-STYLE STEW

Remove and discard the skin and any fat from the duck breasts. Cut the flesh into bite-size pieces.

Heat half the oil in a large, deep skillet and cook the duck, ham, and chorizo over high heat, stirring frequently, for 5 minutes, or until browned on all sides and seared. Using a slotted spoon, remove from the skillet and set aside.

Add the onion, garlic, celery, and chiles to the skillet and cook over medium heat, stirring frequently, for 5 minutes, or until softened. Add the green bell pepper, then stir in the stock, oregano, tomatoes, and hot pepper sauce.

Bring to a boil, then reduce the heat and return the duck, ham, and chorizo to the skillet. Cover and simmer, stirring occasionally, for 20 minutes, or until the duck and ham are tender.

Serve immediately, garnished with parsley and accompanied by salad greens and rice.

SERVES 4

4 duck breasts, about 5½ oz/ 150 g each

2 tbsp olive oil

8 oz/225 g piece ham, cut into small chunks

8 oz/225 g chorizo, outer casing removed, cut into chunks

1 onion, chopped

3 garlic cloves, chopped

3 celery stalks, chopped

1–2 fresh red chiles, seeded and chopped

1 green bell pepper, seeded and chopped

2½ cups chicken stock

1 tbsp chopped fresh oregano

14 oz/400 g canned chopped tomatoes

1–2 tsp hot pepper sauce, or to taste

chopped fresh parsley, to garnish

salad greens and freshly cooked long-grain rice, to serve

FISH & SEAFOOD

MONKFISH PARCELS

Preheat the oven to 375°F/190°C. Cut 4 large pieces of foil, about 9-inches/23-cm square. Brush lightly with a little of the oil, then divide the zucchini and bell pepper among them.

Rinse the fish fillets under cold running water and pat dry with paper towels. Cut them in half, then put 1 piece on top of each pile of zucchini and bell pepper. Cut the bacon slices in half and lay 3 pieces across each piece of fish. Season to taste with salt and pepper, drizzle over the remaining oil, and close up the packages. Seal tightly, transfer to an ovenproof dish, and bake in the preheated oven for 25 minutes.

Remove from the oven, open each foil package slightly, and serve with pasta and slices of olive bread.

SERVES 4

4 tsp olive oil

2 zucchini, sliced

1 large red bell pepper, peeled, seeded, and cut into strips

2 monkfish fillets, about 4½ oz/125 g each, skin and membrane removed

6 smoked lean bacon slices

salt and pepper

freshly cooked pasta and slices of olive bread, to serve

ROASTED MONKFISH

Preheat the oven to 400°F/200°C. Remove the central bone from the fish if not already removed and make small slits down each fillet. Cut 2 of the garlic cloves into thin slivers and insert into the fish. Place the fish on a sheet of wax paper, season with salt and pepper to taste, and drizzle over 1 tablespoon of the oil. Bring the top edges together. Form into a pleat and fold over, then fold the ends underneath, completely encasing the fish. Set aside.

Put the remaining garlic cloves and all the vegetables into a roasting pan and drizzle with the remaining oil, turning the vegetables so that they are well coated in the oil.

Roast in the preheated oven for 20 minutes, turning occasionally. Put the fish package on top of the vegetables and cook for an additional 15–20 minutes, or until the vegetables are tender and the fish is cooked.

Remove from the oven and open up the package. Cut the monkfish into thick slices. Arrange the vegetables on warmed serving plates, top with the fish slices, and sprinkle with the basil. Serve at once.

SERVES 4

1 lb 8 oz/675 g monkfish tail, skinned

4–5 large garlic cloves, peeled

3 tbsp olive oil

1 onion, cut into wedges

1 small eggplant, about 10½ oz/ 300 g, cut into chunks

1 red bell pepper, seeded, cut into wedges

1 yellow bell pepper, seeded, cut into wedges

1 large zucchini, about 8 oz/225 g, cut into wedges

salt and pepper

1 tbsp shredded fresh basil, to garnish

FISH STEW
WITH CIDER

Melt the butter in a large saucepan over medium–low heat. Add the leek and shallots and cook for about 5 minutes, stirring frequently, until they start to soften. Add the cider and bring to a boil.

Stir in the stock, potatoes, and bay leaf with a large pinch of salt (unless stock is salty) and bring back to a boil. Reduce the heat, cover, and cook gently for 10 minutes.

Put the flour in a small bowl and very slowly whisk in a few tablespoons of the milk to make a thick paste. Stir in a little more to make a smooth liquid.

Adjust the heat so the soup bubbles gently. Stir in the flour mixture and cook, stirring frequently, for 5 minutes. Add the remaining milk and half the cream. Continue cooking for about 10 minutes until the potatoes are tender.

Chop the sorrel finely and combine with the remaining cream. Stir the sorrel cream into the stew and add the fish. Continue cooking, stirring occasionally, for about 3 minutes, until the monkfish stiffens or the cod just begins to flake. Taste the stew and adjust the seasoning, if needed. Ladle into warmed bowls, remove the bay leaf, and serve.

SERVES 4

2 tsp butter

1 large leek, thinly sliced

2 shallots, finely chopped

½ cup hard cider

1¼ cups fish stock

9 oz/250 g potatoes, diced

1 bay leaf

4 tbsp all-purpose flour

¾ cup milk

¾ cup heavy cream

2 oz/55 g fresh sorrel leaves

12 oz/350 g skinless monkfish or cod fillet, cut into 1-inch/2.5-cm pieces

salt and pepper

FISH STEW
WITH CIDER

Melt the butter in a large saucepan over medium–low heat. Add the leek and shallots and cook for about 5 minutes, stirring frequently, until they start to soften. Add the cider and bring to a boil.

Stir in the stock, potatoes, and bay leaf with a large pinch of salt (unless stock is salty) and bring back to a boil. Reduce the heat, cover, and cook gently for 10 minutes.

Put the flour in a small bowl and very slowly whisk in a few tablespoons of the milk to make a thick paste. Stir in a little more to make a smooth liquid.

Adjust the heat so the soup bubbles gently. Stir in the flour mixture and cook, stirring frequently, for 5 minutes. Add the remaining milk and half the cream. Continue cooking for about 10 minutes until the potatoes are tender.

Chop the sorrel finely and combine with the remaining cream. Stir the sorrel cream into the stew and add the fish. Continue cooking, stirring occasionally, for about 3 minutes, until the monkfish stiffens or the cod just begins to flake. Taste the stew and adjust the seasoning, if needed. Ladle into warmed bowls, remove the bay leaf, and serve.

SERVES 4

2 tsp butter

1 large leek, thinly sliced

2 shallots, finely chopped

½ cup hard cider

1¼ cups fish stock

9 oz/250 g potatoes, diced

1 bay leaf

4 tbsp all-purpose flour

¾ cup milk

¾ cup heavy cream

2 oz/55 g fresh sorrel leaves

12 oz/350 g skinless monkfish or cod fillet, cut into 1-inch/2.5-cm pieces

salt and pepper

SICILIAN-STYLE TUNA

Whisk all the marinade ingredients together in a small bowl.
Put the tuna steaks in a large, shallow dish and spoon over
4 tablespoons of the marinade, turning until well coated. Cover
and let marinate in the refrigerator for 30 minutes. Set aside the
remaining marinade.

Heat a stovetop ridged grill pan over high heat. Put the fennel
and onions in a separate bowl, add the oil, and toss well to coat.
Add to the grill pan and cook for 5 minutes on each side until just
beginning to color. Transfer to 4 warmed serving plates, drizzle
with the reserved marinade, and keep warm.

Add the tuna steaks to the grill pan and cook, turning once, for
4–5 minutes until firm to the touch but still moist inside. Transfer
the tuna to the serving plates and serve at once with crusty rolls.

SERVES 4

4 tuna steaks, about 5 oz/
140 g each

2 fennel bulbs, thickly sliced
lengthwise

2 red onions, sliced

2 tbsp extra virgin olive oil

crusty rolls, to serve

marinade

½ cup extra virgin olive oil

4 garlic cloves, finely chopped

4 fresh red chiles, seeded and
finely chopped

juice and finely grated rind of
2 lemons

4 tbsp finely chopped fresh
flat-leaf parsley

salt and pepper

MEDITERRANEAN SWORDFISH

SERVES 4

2 tbsp olive oil

1 onion, finely chopped

1 celery stalk, finely chopped

4 oz/115 g green olives, pitted

1 lb/450 g tomatoes, chopped

3 tbsp bottled capers, drained

4 swordfish steaks, about
  5 oz/140 g each

salt and pepper

fresh flat-leaf parsley sprigs,
  to garnish

Heat the oil in a large, heavy-bottom skillet. Add the onion and celery and cook over low heat, stirring occasionally, for 5 minutes, or until softened.

Meanwhile, coarsely chop half the olives. Stir the chopped and whole olives into the pan with the tomatoes and capers and season to taste with salt and pepper.

Bring to a boil, then reduce the heat, cover, and simmer gently, stirring occasionally, for 15 minutes.

Add the swordfish steaks to the pan and return to a boil. Cover and simmer, turning the fish once, for 20 minutes, or until the fish is cooked and the flesh flakes easily. Transfer the fish to serving plates and spoon the sauce over them. Garnish with parsley and serve immediately.

CATALAN FISH STEW

SERVES 4–6

large pinch of saffron threads

4 tbsp almost boiling water

6 tbsp olive oil

1 large onion, chopped

2 garlic cloves, finely chopped

1½ tbsp chopped fresh thyme leaves

2 bay leaves

2 red bell peppers, seeded and coarsely chopped

1 lb 12 oz/800 g canned chopped tomatoes

1 tsp smoked paprika

1 cup fish stock

1 cup blanched almonds, toasted and finely ground

12–16 live mussels

12–16 live clams

1 lb 5 oz/600 g thick boned hake or cod fillets, skinned and cut into 2-inch/5-cm chunks

12–16 raw shrimp, shelled and deveined

salt and pepper

thick crusty bread, to serve

Put the saffron threads in a heatproof pitcher with the water and set aside for at least 10 minutes to infuse.

Heat the oil in a large, heavy-bottom flameproof casserole over medium-high heat. Reduce the heat to low and cook the onion, stirring occasionally, for 10 minutes, or until golden but not browned. Stir in the garlic, thyme, bay leaves, and red bell peppers and cook, stirring frequently, for 5 minutes, or until the bell peppers are softened and the onions have softened further.

Add the tomatoes and paprika and simmer, stirring frequently, for an additional 5 minutes.

Stir in the stock, the saffron and its soaking liquid, and the almonds and bring to a boil, stirring. Reduce the heat and simmer for 5–10 minutes, or until the sauce reduces and thickens. Season to taste with salt and pepper.

Meanwhile, clean the mussels and clams by scrubbing or scraping the shells and pulling out any beards that are attached to the mussels. Discard any with broken shells or any that refuse to close when tapped.

Gently stir the hake into the stew so that it doesn't break up, then add the shrimp, mussels, and clams. Reduce the heat to very low, then cover and simmer for 5 minutes, or until the hake is opaque, the mussels and clams have opened, and the shrimp have turned pink. Discard any mussels or clams that remain closed. Remove the bay leaf and serve immediately with plenty of thick crusty bread for soaking up the juices.

MEDITERRANEAN FISH STEW

Heat the oil in a large, flameproof casserole. Add the onion, saffron, thyme, and a pinch of salt. Cook over low heat, stirring occasionally, for 5 minutes, or until the onion has softened.

Add the garlic and cook for an additional 2 minutes, then add the drained tomatoes and pour in the stock and wine. Season to taste with salt and pepper, bring the mixture to a boil, then reduce the heat and simmer for 15 minutes.

Add the chunks of red snapper and monkfish and simmer for 3 minutes. Add the clams and squid and simmer for 5 minutes, or until the clam shells have opened. Discard any clams that remain closed. Tear in the basil and stir. Serve garnished with the extra basil leaves.

SERVES 4

2 tbsp olive oil

1 onion, sliced

pinch of saffron threads, lightly crushed

1 tbsp chopped fresh thyme

2 garlic cloves, finely chopped

1 lb 12 oz/800 g canned chopped tomatoes, drained

8 cups fish stock

¾ cup dry white wine

12 oz/350 g red snapper or pompano fillets, cut into chunks

1 lb/450 g monkfish fillet, cut into chunks

1 lb/450 g fresh clams, scrubbed

8 oz/225 g squid rings

2 tbsp fresh basil leaves, plus extra to garnish

salt and pepper

SHRIMP LAKSA

Shell and devein the shrimp. Put the fish stock, salt, and the shrimp heads, shells, and tails in a large saucepan over high heat and slowly bring to a boil. Lower the heat and simmer for 10 minutes, then remove from the heat. Transfer to a bowl and keep warm

Meanwhile, make the laksa paste. Put all the ingredients except the oil in a food processor and blend. With the motor running, slowly add up to 2 tablespoons of oil just until a paste forms. (If your food processor is too large to work efficiently with this small quantity, use a mortar and pestle, or make double the quantity and keep leftovers tightly covered in the refrigerator to use another time.)

Heat the oil in the cleaned large saucepan over high heat. Add the paste and stir-fry until it is fragrant. Strain the stock through a strainer lined with cheesecloth. Stir the stock into the laksa paste, along with the coconut milk, nam pla, and lime juice. Bring to a boil, then lower the heat, cover, and simmer for 30 minutes.

Meanwhile, soak the noodles in a large bowl with enough lukewarm water to cover for 20 minutes, until soft. Alternatively, cook according to the package instructions. Drain and set aside.

Add the shrimp and bean sprouts to the soup and continue simmering just until the shrimp turn opaque and curl. Divide the noodles among 4 bowls and ladle the soup over, making sure everyone gets an equal share of the shrimp. Garnish with the cilantro and serve.

SERVES 4

20–24 large raw unshelled shrimp

2 cups fish stock

pinch of salt

1 tsp peanut oil

2 cups coconut milk

2 tsp nam pla (Thai fish sauce)

½ tbsp lime juice

4 oz/115 g dried medium rice noodles

⅜ cup bean sprouts

sprigs of fresh cilantro, to garnish

laksa paste

6 fresh cilantro stalks with leaves

3 large garlic cloves, crushed

1 fresh red chile, seeded and chopped

1 lemongrass stalk, center part only, chopped

1-inch/2.5-cm piece fresh ginger, peeled and chopped

1½ tbsp shrimp paste

½ tsp ground turmeric

2 tbsp peanut oil

ROASTED
SEAFOOD

SERVES 4

1 lb 5 oz/600 g new potatoes, scrubbed and parboiled for 10–15 minutes

3 red onions, cut into wedges

2 zucchini, cut into chunks

8 garlic cloves, peeled but left whole

2 lemons, cut into wedges

4 fresh rosemary sprigs

4 tbsp olive oil

12 oz/350 g unshelled raw shrimp

2 small raw squid, cut into rings

4 tomatoes, quartered

Preheat the oven to 400°F/200°C. Place the potatoes in a large roasting pan together with the onions, zucchini, garlic, lemons, and rosemary sprigs.

Pour over the oil and toss to coat all the vegetables in it. Roast in the oven for 30 minutes, turning occasionally, until the potatoes are tender.

Once the potatoes are tender, add the shrimp, squid, and tomatoes, tossing to coat them in the oil, and roast for 10 minutes. All the vegetables should be cooked through and slightly charred for full flavor. Transfer the roasted seafood and vegetables to warmed serving plates and serve hot.

SEAFOOD IN SAFFRON SAUCE

Clean the mussels and clams by scrubbing or scraping the shells and pulling out any beards that are attached to the mussels. Discard any with broken shells or any that refuse to close when tapped.

Heat the oil in a large, flameproof casserole and cook the onion with the saffron, thyme, and a pinch of salt over low heat, stirring occasionally, for 5 minutes, or until softened.

Add the garlic and cook, stirring, for 2 minutes. Add the tomatoes, wine, and stock, then season to taste with salt and pepper and stir well. Bring to a boil, then reduce the heat and simmer for 15 minutes.

Add the fish chunks and simmer for an additional 3 minutes. Add the mussels, clams, and squid rings and simmer for an additional 5 minutes, or until the mussels and clams have opened. Discard any that remain closed. Stir in the basil and serve immediately, accompanied by plenty of fresh bread to soak up the broth.

SERVES 4

8 oz/225 g live mussels

8 oz/225 g live clams

2 tbsp olive oil

1 onion, sliced

pinch of saffron threads

1 tbsp chopped fresh thyme

2 garlic cloves, finely chopped

1 lb 12 oz/800 g canned tomatoes, drained and chopped

¾ cup dry white wine

8 cups fish stock

12 oz/350 g red snapper fillets, cut into bite-size chunks

1 lb/450 g monkfish fillet, cut into bite-size chunks

8 oz/225 g raw squid rings

2 tbsp fresh shredded basil leaves

salt and pepper

fresh bread, to serve

SEAFOOD CHILI

Place the shrimp, scallops, monkfish chunks, and lime slices in a large, nonmetallic dish with ¼ teaspoon of the chili powder, ¼ teaspoon of the ground cumin, 1 tablespoon of the chopped cilantro, half the garlic, the fresh chile, and 1 tablespoon of the oil. Cover with plastic wrap and let marinate for up to 1 hour.

Meanwhile, heat 1 tablespoon of the remaining oil in a flameproof casserole or large, heavy-bottom pan. Add the onion, the remaining garlic, and the red and yellow bell peppers and cook over low heat, stirring occasionally, for 5 minutes, or until softened.

Add the remaining chili powder, the remaining cumin, the cloves, cinnamon, and cayenne, with the remaining oil if necessary, and season to taste with salt. Cook, stirring, for 5 minutes, then gradually stir in the stock and the tomatoes and their juices. Partially cover and simmer for 25 minutes.

Add the beans to the tomato mixture and spoon the fish and shellfish on top. Cover and cook for 10 minutes, or until the fish and shellfish are cooked through. Sprinkle with the remaining cilantro and serve.

SERVES 4

4 oz/115 g raw shrimp, peeled

9 oz/250 g prepared scallops, thawed if frozen

4 oz/115 g monkfish fillet, cut into chunks

1 lime, peeled and thinly sliced

1 tbsp chili powder

1 tsp ground cumin

3 tbsp chopped fresh cilantro

2 garlic cloves, finely chopped

1 fresh green chile, seeded and chopped

3 tbsp corn oil

1 onion, coarsely chopped

1 red and 1 yellow pepper, seeded and coarsely chopped

¼ tsp ground cloves

pinch of ground cinnamon

pinch of cayenne pepper

salt

1½ cups fish stock

14 oz/400 g canned chopped tomatoes

14 oz/400 g canned red kidney beans, drained and rinsed

GOAN-STYLE SEAFOOD CURRY

Heat the oil in a wok or large skillet over high heat. Add the mustard seeds and stir them around for about 1 minute, or until they jump. Stir in the curry leaves.

Add the shallots and garlic and stir for about 5 minutes, or until the shallots are golden. Stir in the turmeric, coriander, and chili powder and continue stirring for about 30 seconds.

Add the dissolved creamed coconut. Bring to a boil, then reduce the heat to medium and stir for about 2 minutes.

Reduce the heat to low, add the fish, and simmer for 1 minute, spooning the sauce over the fish and very gently stirring it around. Add the shrimp and continue to simmer for an additional 4–5 minutes until the fish flesh flakes easily and the shrimp turn pink and curl.

Add half the lime juice, then taste and add more lime juice and salt to taste. Sprinkle with the lime rind and serve with lime slices.

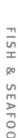

SERVES 4–6

3 tbsp vegetable oil or peanut oil

1 tbsp black mustard seeds

12 fresh curry leaves or 1 tbsp dried

6 shallots, finely chopped

1 garlic clove, crushed

1 tsp ground turmeric

½ ground coriander

¼–½ tsp chili powder

5 oz/140 g creamed coconut, grated and dissolved in 1¼ cups boiling water

1 lb 2 oz/500 g skinless, boneless white fish, such as monkfish or cod, cut into large chunks

1 lb/450 g large raw shrimp, shelled and deveined

juice and finely grated rind of 1 lime

salt

lime slices, to serve

VEGETABLES

RATATOUILLE

Coarsely chop the eggplants and zucchini, and seed and chop the bell peppers. Slice the onions and finely chop the garlic. Heat the oil in a large skillet. Add the onions and cook over low heat, stirring occasionally, for 5 minutes, or until softened. Add the garlic and cook, stirring frequently for an additional 2 minutes.

Add the eggplants, zucchini, and bell peppers. Increase the heat to medium and cook, stirring occasionally, until the bell peppers begin to color. Add the bouquet garni, reduce the heat, cover, and simmer gently for 40 minutes.

Stir in the chopped tomatoes and season to taste with salt and pepper. Re-cover the pan and simmer gently for an additional 10 minutes. Remove and discard the bouquet garni. Serve warm or cold.

SERVES 4

2 medium-size eggplants

4 zucchini

2 yellow bell peppers

2 red bell peppers

2 onions

2 garlic cloves

⅔ cup olive oil

1 bouquet garni

3 large tomatoes, peeled, seeded, and coarsely chopped

salt and pepper

ROASTED SUMMER VEGETABLES

Brush an ovenproof dish with a little oil. Arrange the fennel, onions, tomatoes, eggplant, zucchini, and bell peppers in the dish and tuck the garlic cloves and rosemary sprigs among them. Drizzle with the remaining oil and season to taste with pepper.

Roast the vegetables in a preheated oven, 400°F/200°C, for 10 minutes. Turn the vegetables over, return the dish to the oven, and roast for an additional 10–15 minutes or until the vegetables are tender and beginning to turn golden brown.

Serve the vegetables straight from the dish or transfer to a warm serving platter. Serve immediately, with crusty bread, if using, to soak up the juices.

SERVES 4

2 tbsp olive oil

1 fennel bulb, cut into wedges

2 red onions, cut into wedges

2 beefsteak tomatoes, cut into wedges

1 eggplant, thickly sliced

2 zucchini, thickly sliced

1 yellow bell pepper, seeded and cut into chunks

1 red bell pepper, seeded and cut into chunks

1 orange bell pepper, seeded and cut into chunks

4 garlic cloves

4 fresh rosemary sprigs

ground black pepper

crusty bread, to serve (optional)

POTATO & MUSHROOM PIE

SERVES 4

2 tbsp butter

1 lb/450 g waxy potatoes, thinly sliced and parboiled

2 cups sliced mixed mushrooms

1 tbsp chopped rosemary

4 tbsp snipped chives, plus extra to garnish

2 garlic cloves, crushed

²/₃ cup heavy cream

salt and pepper

Grease a shallow round ovenproof dish with butter.

Layer a quarter of the potatoes in the bottom of the dish. Arrange a quarter of the mushrooms on top of the potatoes and sprinkle with a quarter of the rosemary, chives, and garlic. Continue making layers in the same order, finishing with a layer of potatoes on top.

Pour the heavy cream over the top of the potatoes. Season to taste with salt and pepper.

Cook in a preheated oven, 375°F/190°C, for about 45 minutes or until the pie is golden brown on top and piping hot.

Garnish with snipped chives and serve at once straight from the dish.

VEGETABLES

227

EGGPLANT GRATIN

Heat the oil in a flameproof casserole over medium heat. Add the onions and cook for 5 minutes or until soft. Add the garlic and cook for a few seconds or until just beginning to color. Using a slotted spoon, transfer the onion mixture to a plate.

Cook the eggplant slices in batches in the same flameproof casserole until they are just lightly browned. Transfer to another plate.

Preheat the oven to 400°F/200°C. Arrange a layer of eggplant slices in the bottom of the casserole dish. Sprinkle with the parsley, thyme, and salt and pepper.

Add a layer of onion, tomatoes, and mozzarella, sprinkling parsley, thyme, and salt and pepper over each layer.

Continue layering, finishing with a layer of eggplant slices. Sprinkle with the Parmesan. Bake, uncovered, for 20–30 minutes or until the top is golden and the eggplants are tender. Serve hot.

SERVES 2

4 tbsp olive oil

2 onions, finely chopped

2 garlic cloves, very finely chopped

2 eggplants, thickly sliced

3 tbsp fresh flat-leaf parsley, chopped

½ tsp dried thyme

14 oz/400 g canned chopped tomatoes

1½ cups coarsely grated mozzarella

6 tbsp freshly grated Parmesan

salt and pepper